CHRIST AN

THE 21ST CENTURY IN OUR TIME SERIES

Series Editor: Anne Mathews-Younes, Ed.D., D.Min.
Managing Editor: Shivraj K. Mahendra, Ph.D.

First Edition, July, 1933
Second Printing, July, 1933
Third Printing, August, 1933
Fourth Printing, September, 1933
Filth Printing, October, 1933
Sixth Printing, October, 1933
Seventh Printing, December, 1933
Eighth Printing, October, 1934
Ninth Printing, December, 1936
Tenth Printing, March, 1937
Eleventh Printing, Revised edition, December, 2020

CHRIST AND HUMAN SUFFERING

Revised Edition

E. STANLEY JONES

CHRIST AND HUMAN SUFFERING
by E. Stanley Jones

First published by Abingdon Press, 1933

The 21st Century in Our Times Series

Printed and published with permission by
The E. Stanley Jones Foundation
Email: anne@estanleyjonesfoundation.com
www.estanleyjonesfoundation.com

Cover design: Marc Whitaker
Interior design: Shivraj K. Mahendra

ISBN: 9798690150532

MANUFACTURED IN THE USA

DEDICATION

With great appreciation and deep respect for the courage, commitment, and sacrifice of the countless men and women who brave daily challenges as first responders and

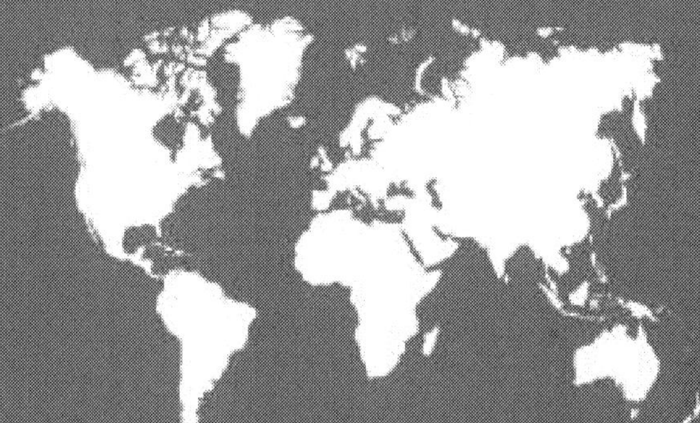

front line workers who risk their lives to save the lives of others, and protect public safety and health throughout the COVID-19 Pandemic. We honor and celebrate these heroes among us, as they extend care to relieve human suffering.

- *Editor*

CONTENTS

PREFACE

C*hrist and Human Suffering* offers a positive and active way to deal with sorrow. This is a particularly significant book for our current pandemic crisis, where we are challenged by personal and collective suffering as a result of COVID-19's march across our world. Jones' book moves beyond answering the "why" questions we so often ask of suffering and on to sharing just "how" suffering can be used to further personal transformation. Jones affirms that we can *make our sorrows contribute to transforming ourselves and others.*

This view of suffering is nothing less than the power to take suffering up into the purpose of our lives and transmute it into character and achievement. "This is no mere philosophy of life. It is the very essence of the Christian faith." (p. 206). According to Jones, the idea that the Christian faith offers escape from suffering is completely foreign to that faith. The Christian shares with the rest of humanity the ills incident to life in a world of this kind – death of loved ones, loss of health, loss of friendships, disappointments in love, the nonfulfillment of ambitions, the frustrations that come from living in an unfinished world. In an unfinished world we are bound to meet up with things that gall us, and if we let them they will break us.

That is his point— "if we let them." (p. 206). Our reactions to these things largely determine the result. It is not what happens to you, but what you do with it, after it does happen, that determines the result. The same thing happens to two people, one it makes bitter, the other it makes better. Our inner attitude determines the result.

Jones continues, "There is a saying, 'When Fate throws a dagger at you, there are two ways to catch it: either by the blade or by the handle.'" Fate is bound to throw a dagger at you, no one will be spared. "Whether we grasp it by the blade and let it cut us to the quick, or whether we grasp it by the handle and make it an instrument of defense depends on the inner spirit." (p. 209) According to Jones, our reaction determines the result.

> When life threw a cross at Jesus, Jesus took hold of that worst thing that could happen to Him and made it into the best thing that could happen to the world. The cross was sin, pure, unadulterated sin and Jesus turned it into the healing of sin. The cross was hate, and Jesus turned it into a revelation of love. The cross represented life speaking its darkest, cruelest word, and Jesus turned it into God speaking His most redemptive word**. Jesus did not bear the cross, Jesus used it!** A religion with a cross at its center doesn't offer mere comfort, a drying of tears, it offers a moral and spiritual mastery that turns sorrow into song and a crucifixion into an Easter morning. (p. 209)

United Methodist Bishop Bruce R. Ough also affirms, through experience, that God's last word is not the cross, but the resurrection. Bishop Ough writes, "I first read *Christ and Human Suffering* shortly after witnessing my parents' debilitating anguish following the death of their 20 year old son (my brother) from heart disease. E. Stanley Jones saved me from a limited and limiting understanding of both personal and corporate suffering and tragedy and set me on a path of understanding "God's last word is not the cross, but the resurrection." This has become the touchstone of my call and my ministry. *Christ and Human Suffering* is a timeless book. We have all known or witnessed suffering; it is a part and parcel of life in every age in every place. This classic work of E. Stanley Jones is a must read for every pastor, politician, philosopher, physician and prophet.

Ashram leader Denton Florian comments, "The problem of human suffering is the most difficult theological question and Stanley Jones wades right into the middle of it. He does not fall back on cliches or sugar coat suffering. Christ demonstrated a 'working way to live' and Jones challenges us to consider and apply it in our daily lives. *Christ and Human Suffering* is a powerfully enlightening book and I believe is the best resource that is available on human suffering from a Christian viewpoint."

This book has also been graced by commentaries from United Methodist Pastor, Mark Suter, who emphasizes that the Christian way of meeting suffering is not merely enduring it, but making it serve the higher purpose of the Kingdom of God. He adds that the current Covid-19 crisis presents today's church and all of us with both a problem and a possibility. Let's grasp the possibility!

Dr. Zac Varghese, a physician, writes that this book is not just about living with individual sufferings—innocent, self-inflicted or inflicted by other agencies; it is about dealing with personal suffering and having empathy and compassion for the suffering of others by growing with Jesus Christ in overcoming them. Dr. Varghese writes, "I have dealt with pain and suffering all of my professional life—yet gained a more profound understanding of suffering from this book. It is a good companion for all of us and particularly for those who are involved in the ministry of healing."

God is present with us in this pandemic moment as we open our eyes to a world of hurting neighbors and offer our love and connection to a world in need of God's love through us. This is what we can do with suffering. We don't bear it, we use it to serve others.

Blessings on you dear reader!

ANNE MATHEWS-YOUNES
December 2020

FOREWORD

My first E. Stanley Jones book was a well-worn paperback copy of "Abundant Living" I borrowed from my father's bookshelf. As a young student pastor, I was drawn like a magnet to the simple, yet profound, expression of the gospel, the Kingdom of God, and Jesus, the Word made flesh. I felt that I had touched middle C or found the answer key to life—Jesus. Just Jesus—not a Bible story, a theology, not a church or religion, but the very essence of reality itself. In Jones, I had discovered worldview thinking long before I knew what it was.

But what does a young pastor do when life isn't all that "abundant"? When called to mediate a crumbling marriage? When a mother weeps over a wayward son and asks why? When a husband and wife are killed instantly in a head-on collision on the way to Sunday dinner? When a pillar of the church drifts away into dementia? When a young mother loses a long battle with cancer? When suffering souls look to you for answers and you know you're in over your head?

Perhaps that's why this book was one of Jones's earliest. As all pastors soon discover, that the question of suffering, or what C. S.

Lewis called the "problem of pain," is inescapable. Does the Christ of the Indian road, the Christ of every road, and the Christ of the Mount really know the road of suffering that everyone travels sooner or later?

Before there's any abundant living, the question of suffering and pain would have to be faced. "Did the Christian gospel have a clear answer?" Jones asks. "And one that would work?" As with all his writing, he determined not to "write this book as theory. It must be a working way to live."

Thus, *Christ and Human Suffering* is not a simplistic three-step solution or a resolution of competing theologies. Stanley Jones would never settle for "the Word become word."We must instead have something actual and adequate to offer men and women and children sinking in stress, sickness, struggle, and suffering. Will our gospel be truly "good news" or turn out to be only "good views"? Is it the Word become word or the Word made Flesh? Is it just one of many equally valid options, or is it the only workable way to live in this world? Is it merely "a" way, or is it "the" Way?

The only way to know the answer to this question is to "put it under life," even in the hardest places and the darkest moments of life. We cannot live on answers that "keep the word of promise to our ears and break it to our hope."

The gospel more than meets the challenge and life's demand. God spoke his clearest word in the Word made Flesh, in Jesus. Jesus took on all that humanity is and does and knows, even full identification with the sin and suffering of humankind, even numbering himself with all transgressors at the cross.

The method of Jesus, however, was not just to endure or bravely bear suffering as a martyr, but to take the absolute worst and make it serve his ultimate purpose—the redemption of fallen men and women. Just so, the only way to take the sting and pain out of life's inevitable suffering and struggle is to transform it and use it for a higher purpose in the same way God met our wounds in the wounds of Jesus, the Son—using the worst man could do to achieve the most God could do.

Christ and Human Suffering, then, is not so much an answer to a question as a way through a wilderness—a "working way to live." It is the way of so many faithful saints and seekers I have known and admired over my years of ministry.

A woman virtually homebound with arthritis could not straighten out her fingers and labored mightily just to get across a room. Several of her joints had been surgically replaced. But when asked, she never failed to smile and answer, "I'm doing just fine!" And she was, in spite of. She turned her pain and limitation into a powerful prayer partner and card writing ministry—and was even able to type.

In a testimony service at Thanksgiving, a husband and wife began by giving praise and thanks to God with a genuine smile from hearts overflowing with God's Spirit, made even more remarkable by the knowledge that their daughter and two grandchildren, had, some years earlier, been killed in a car crash.

A woman found herself alone and abandoned by an unfaithful husband, yet today is a powerful prayer warrior, still serves on mission teams around the world, and has led many to faith in Christ through her "overcoming" witness.

A church leader with an exceptional gift of encouragement was taken down by cancer and given just a short time to live. His last days saw a steady procession of so many coming to thank him for lifting them up and to witness the victorious way he faced sickness, treatment, and decline, and to the last giving away more than anyone could ever repay.

I think of a young pastor and wife who traveled this road of making pain and suffering serve a higher purpose. Their life's challenge was a daughter born with severe physical and mental handicaps. Their journey became a testimony of the Spirit of Christ shining through their brokenness, living the gospel as much as preaching it. Along the way, she spoke with Stanley Jones at an Ashram, who counseled surrender and trust in God's larger purposes. Part of those larger purposes was their influence and mentoring of my parents in their early Christian walk, part of which was a gift of Jones's book, *How to Be a Transformed Person*. It became the beginning of my precious collection of all of Jones's books and my conviction that his grasp of the timeless truth of Jesus is still true and cries out to be heard in our time.

It is not at all surprising, then, that this reissue of *Christ and Human Suffering* comes as the world is grappling with the devastating effects of the COVID-19 pandemic. E. Stanley Jones had the gift of articulating the distinction between the eternal and the temporal, the universal and the particular, the unchanging and the unpredictable, and the Kingdom of God and the Christian Church. So it is, *Christ and Human Suffering* that speaks hope and possibility, even in a worldwide pandemic, decades after he wrote this book.

If the Christian way of meeting suffering is not merely enduring it, but making it serve the higher purpose of the Kingdom of God, then the current COVID-19 crisis presents today's church with both a problem and a possibility.

The sudden emergence of an invisible, insidious virus of unknown scope and severity came as a shock to the system, both personally and corporately. Churches were suddenly closed and declared forbidden zones. Any sense of community and togetherness was shattered as we shuttered within our homes. Mere survival was, for a time, an open question.

For the Church, along with its pastors, the enforced isolation and extended closures have become a defining moment, forcing us back upon the first questions of faith and life. Who am I? What do I really believe? Who am I trusting? What are we living for?

Who are we together when we cannot even be together? How do we function as the church of Christ amid suffering, fear, and isolation? How do we care for the sick and hurting among us? What can we offer a world grasping for answers? What does a preacher do without a congregation?

As Paul reluctantly learned, with his thorn in the flesh, the prolonged pain of the pandemic may not be soon eased or eliminated. The Church has been profoundly, and likely permanently, changed.

However, *Christ and Human Suffering* still speaks across the years if COVID-19 calls us back to who we are in Christ and what we are called to do. Are we still the church when we cannot gather to sing, pray, and worship? Is the gospel still good news in a hurting world? Do we still serve a risen Savior even when church doors are closed on Easter Sunday? For those who surrender to the unchanging Christ at the head of an unshakable Kingdom, to ask it is to answer it.

The soul-searching shaking of a global pandemic of unknown origin and extent can become the church's finest hour. It can draw us to deeper devotion to the person of Christ apart from the program of one's church. It can shake us out of the doldrums of church maintenance and forever majoring on the minors. It can unite the Body of Christ as we long for the touch and closeness we are missing.

It can open our eyes to a world of hurting neighbors and hungry souls just beyond the walls of our buildings and sanctuaries. It can ignite healthy change and creativity in how we communicate and connect with an online world. It can open new doors for our gospel of hope and transformation.

Unless suffering is allowed the last word, even a painful season of purifying and pruning can be taken up into God's larger work of making his Church even more fruitful and molding his people into the likeness of Christ.

This is a book for our time because the questions and the heartache of suffering and pain are perennial and eternal. With great understatement did Jesus tell us ahead of time, "In the world you will have trouble." Our own stories, tragedies, hurts, doubts, fears, unanswered prayers, and unanswered questions would fill many pages.

But it is also for our time because what Jones offers here is nothing more or less than the overcoming gospel of Jesus Christ, the crucified and risen One, the unchanging Person and Lord of an unshakable Kingdom. "Be of good cheer; I have overcome the world."

Mark Suter
United Methodist Pastor

INTRODUCTION

In the midst of my work in that vast continent of suffering, China, I was forced to face anew, before my audiences, the question of human suffering, merited and unmerited. How could one escape it? The Chinese face masks more than it reveals, but even it could not hide the throbbing pains within. Their nation was in bitter travail; was it birth pangs or death throes? It was difficult to say. Many alternated between hope and despair.

Besides this great national pain, each life seemed to hold some personal pain, often too deep for words. Usually they held it in check, but sometimes, unable to suppress it any longer, they blurted it out, as did one highly intellectual man, the head of a great university, in one of our Round Table Conferences: "I am lost. I cannot see my way. I have been looking for someone to talk to. I do not mind whether his advice is good or bad, I must talk to someone. I can hold my trouble no longer." His son, a student in college, had recently died by suicide as a result of brooding over his country's troubles.

In such a situation how could one escape facing human pain? Did the Christian gospel have a clear answer? And is it one that would work? If so, what was it? I tried to interpret the Christian answer and to show the way out. In one of the series of meetings a missionary lady, so badly crippled from childhood arthritis that she had constantly to use crutches, wrote to me this brief note: "Please write your next book on glorying in infirmities, I am!" That week she had seen what to her was a new way; life had been transformed and she was radiant. I smiled at the request, and promptly forgot it, for I had been collecting material for several years for another book on another subject and that task occupied the field. But on my way to that other continent of suffering, India, I stopped at Singapore and, while speaking to an audience there on this matter of meeting suffering in a Christian way, it suddenly flashed through my mind that this was the subject for the next book. It seemed not a vagrant thought to be pushed aside as interfering with one in the midst of an address, but an illumination from outside, one, so clear, so imperious and so compelling. When I returned later to the subject of the book on which I was working, it wasn't there. This new topic held the field. It possessed me.

When I looked around at the outer facts, they seemed to fit the inward illumination. The more I thought on the matter, the more was I convinced that on scarcely anything else is Christendom more confused, more pathetically tangled than on this matter of suffering and the way to meet it. But if Christendom is confused, then non-Christendom is more so. The suffering seems worldwide, and one of the most poignant elements in that suffering is that so many see no real significance in it. It all seems so senseless, leading nowhere. Or if they do see any meaning in it, that meaning seems to be a sinister one, namely, that this is a world of unfeeling chance. There is no Heart behind it. The pathetic thing is that many see no clear way out. Most people are just muddling through, or not getting through at all, they are left stranded amid a sea of troubles. Certainly, if anyone had any light on such a subject, now was the time to share it.

But to write on such a subject is to walk on holy ground, hallowed by the tears and blood stained footsteps of many a wearied one. To bungle here would be serious. To raise hopes in a suffering heart that could not be fulfilled would only add pain to pain. I hesitated. But objection after objection seemed to be swept away, and I came to my final condition and took my stand there, refusing to go on unless I could be assured at this point: "I cannot write this book as theory. It must be a working way to live. I have learned something of this Secret, and it has been glorious; but I can write on this subject only on one condition, that you teach me, Father, to walk in this way, and to walk in it with abandon, as I try to unfold it to others." He promised. Then, so did I. We will walk together, then, in a common quest.

E. STANLEY JONES

1

THE CONFUSION

I spoke of India and China being the "continents of suffering," but can we stop there? Is not every person at some time or other involved in this common human suffering? The gentle Buddha, brooding long and deeply over life, came to a conclusion that fairly takes our breath away. It was this: Existence and suffering are one. As long as we are bound to the wheel of existence we are bound to suffer, for existence and suffering are one, not accidentally or incidentally, but intrinsically and inescapably. The only way to get out of suffering is to get out of existence itself. What a startling, breathtaking, one might almost say, life-taking conclusion to come to! And yet hundreds of millions of our human brothers repeat that for a creed as day by day they say: "*Ameisa, Duklca, Annath,*" "Impermanence, Suffering, Emptiness."

The conclusion is more thoroughgoing but not startlingly different from that of the writer of Ecclesiastes when he says: "I have seen all the works that are done under the sun; and, behold, all is vanity and a striving after wind." In the book of Job it is said,

For affliction cometh not forth of the dust,
Neither doth trouble spring out of the ground;

But man is born unto trouble,
As the sparks fly upward.

And the book itself was written to deal with this problem of unmerited suffering. Whether the answer found in this ancient book is an adequate one we must study later, but the problem bore down upon the men of that day, as it does of these days and demanded a solution.

A more modern person cries out in these lines: "My son, the world is dark with griefs and graves, So dark that men cry out against the heavens." I suppose there is nothing that makes men and women cry out against the heavens so much as the anguish that comes to the heart unbidden and seemingly unmerited.

A very modern young woman hires an airplane, and when in mid-air steps out into the void, leaving this note behind: "I have had nothing but discord, and I long for harmony. Perhaps I shall find music where I go." She felt that she could not find it in this kind of a world. So, she takes upon herself, the great responsibility and steps out.

Horace Walpole says, "To those who think, life is comedy; to those who feel, life is tragedy." There are few of us who do not "feel." Then, is life a tragedy to all? In Pompeii, the guide will show you the remains of the theater in which only comedies were played, and alongside of it those of the one in which tragedies only were presented. But can comedy and tragedy be separated in life in this way? Do they not flow together in an amazing confusion?

Life at the present time seems to be decidedly tragic, because, first of all, we are passing through an age of sweeping transition. It differs from other ages of transition in that it is deeper and more thoroughgoing. Things upon which men and women had depended, and in which they had trusted and hoped, have gone out from under them. Yesterday, these things were solid, today they are gone, gone except for the lingering pain they leave behind. This is happening, not only in the realm of the material, but in the realm of the spiritual as well. Many have exposed themselves to the breath of modern thinking, with the result that many of their spiritual values have been dissolved. They have not deliberately turned away from them, but have awakened to find them not there. Their absence leaves them with something akin to what French Scholar Ernest Renan experienced when he broke with the church and told of the experience in these words: "The enchanted circle which embraced the whole of life is broken, and the feeling of emptiness is left like that which follows on an attack of fever or an unhappy love affair." The growing distrust of life itself leaves many people empty and confused. As someone has put it, "It [modern culture] has set man on the world's vacant throne; but it can no longer worship its idol. Self-worship is seldom successful. This is the skepticism that is destroying us. Under the garish, flamboyant surface of contemporary Western culture is a growing distrust of life itself." You cannot be happy except in the sum total of things, and many face the gnawing question as to whether the sum total of things has any meaning or purpose.

> *Life at the present time seems to be decidedly tragic, because, first of all, we are passing through an age of sweeping transition.*

Some of our modern suffering comes from this transitional period and some comes from the fact that we are embodied spirits, and must work out our destiny with recalcitrant matter. We have infinite desires and are embodied in a very finite, material world. So, we feel thwarted and cramped and stultified at every turn. It has been said that "the difficulty is not that we are a higher hog and a human soul, but that we are both at one and the same time." The hog side of us loves filthy mud holes and would naturalize us there, but the soul side of us does not really love mud and sets up its protest and cries out to be delivered. It feels the call of the Eternal. This conflict is deadly to happiness.

Once, a fortune teller accosted me, and to catch my attention and to get me into a frame of mind in which I would allow him to tell my fortune, he began by saying: "You seem happy, but it is only outward. In the inside, you are always thinking, thinking about getting something you cannot get. So, you are not happy." I laughed and told him that he had missed it! The fortune teller was shrewd enough to know that the approach would work in most cases. For most people are wearing unseen crosses about which they do not whisper, save in the ears of God, provided, of course, that they can find him. But if they cannot find him, then, they must smother down the choking ache and suffer it, alone.

Besides these sufferings incidental to human living, there come the special calamities that often fall upon us suddenly and leave us stunned and blinded. Today, I picked up my letters, with eagerness, to find out about my daughter's graduation from high school in the Himalayas, an event I had reluctantly to miss, because of my China tour. After describing the happy event, it told of a trip from the mountains toward their homes in the plains, and event always full of joy and bubbling happiness. But not this one! For one of the girls, who also had graduated, turned to wave goodbye to some of her companions on the hills above, stepped backward against a low wall, so she thought; but it proved to be an open space in the wall and down she fell, two hundred feet, to her death. And, she was a widowed mother's only daughter.

Why did this calamity happen to this particular widow so recently bereaved of her husband? Why did it not happen to the daughter of somebody else, mine, for instance? It is here that our problems become acute and baffling. And many are badly confused at this point. In China two missionary children belonging to different families came down with diphtheria at the same time. One child recovered and the other child died. I found the father of the child that had died deeply embittered because his child, an only child, had died, while the other child, belonging to a family in which there were other children, was spared. His faith seemed to slip away from him. Doesn't God answer our prayers in such a case as this and intervene? Some feel that he should, and does. But when he does not, as obviously he does not, then what? The universe tumbles in on one, and faith crashes too. It is at this point that the faith of many suffers its deepest shocks.

In one of our Round Table Conferences in India a fine young Englishman, a leader among the group of business men who wanted better relationships between India and Great Britain, said in rather a disillusioned way: "God let me down. My brother was wounded in the war. I prayed to God that my brother might live. Any decent person would have answered such a prayer. But God didn't, and my brother died. Now I have no faith left. I do think that Christ was the greatest Personality that ever lived. But God let me down, so I have no religion. I wish I did have one."

This question was sent up by a student in China: "My sister was a very godly woman. But she suffered dreadfully in childbirth. Why didn't God spare her this suffering, since she was such a godly woman?"

A professor in a great university in America was struck by a truck, knocked down, and his leg broken. After he recovered, at the first appearance in the chapel service he said to the students: "I no longer believe in a personal God. If there were a personal God, would he not have whispered to me to beware of the danger of the coming truck and have saved me from this calamity?" He was struck down, and in the fall his faith crashed too.

An Indian arose in one of my meetings in India and said: "Since I have become a Christian, I have had no more troubles at all. God has saved me from all my troubles." He sat down with a great deal of satisfaction, for his statement seemed a proof, that God was pleased with him.

Now, here are four illustrations: one from Britain, one from America, one from China, and the fourth from India, all converging on one thought, namely, that God should spare the righteous from trouble. When God does not, it is either a sign that he does not exist, or that, if he does exist, there is something wrong in him or in us. They all agree that if there is a God, he should spare his children from troubles and calamities. In the case of the Indian the fact that God had so far done so was a sign of his special favor.

Isn't there something fundamentally wrong here? Does the gospel teach that if we follow Christ, our child will never be taken away by diphtheria when she is an only child? —That our brothers will not die when wounded in war if we will but pray? –That our sisters, if they are righteous, will not suffer in childbirth? —That God will undertake to whisper a warning to us, his children, when we are about to be knocked down by a truck? And that when he does so intervene and save us from all troubles, it is a special sign of his favor? And that his doing so is proof that religion works? There seems to be something fundamentally wrong here.

Suppose it should be guaranteed that calamities would always strike the wicked alone, and that the righteous would always be saved, what kind of a world would this be? Its laws would always be in process of suspension whenever the righteous were involved. Gravity wouldn't pull you downward even though you leaned too far out over the parapet, provided, of course, you were righteous. What kind of a universe would we soon have? Certainly, not a dependable one, for in a situation about to develop, you would not know whether laws would act, for you would not know the character of the persons involved. You would find out only when the event happened. If the person was good, the law would be suspended; if bad, it would smite him. It would indeed be a very undependable universe. Moreover, what would be the result in the characters of the persons concerned? It would be disastrous.

God has chosen to run the universe by order rather than by whim and notion. The laws are orderly because God's mind is orderly; they are dependable because God is a dependable God.

I do not question that God can and sometimes does intervene and save his children in particular situations, for God certainly cannot be put in a straight jacket in his universe. The laws of the universe are God's habitual way of running that universe, and to say that he cannot do otherwise is to make him less than his modes of action. God has chosen to run the universe by order rather than by whim and notion. The laws are orderly because God's mind is orderly; they are dependable because God is a dependable God. But to say that he cannot do other than he does habitually is to leave us a God who is the victim of his own ways. I believe he can intervene. But what I do object to, is saying that God should intervene in impending calamity whenever his children are concerned; and that when he does so, it is a special sign of his being pleased with the persons involved; and that when he does not, there is something wrong either in God or in them.

The Christian solution of the problem of suffering does not lie along this line. If it did, then the Christian would turn out to be the cosmic pet, and a petted child is always a spoiled child.

When Jesus was hanging on the cross, deserted of men and seemingly of God, the crowd cried out, "He trusted in God; let him deliver him now, if he desires him." If God should deliver him, it would be a proof that Jesus was good and pleasing to God; but if not, then it was sure proof that God did not desire him, so they thought.

God did not deliver him. *But he did something better.* And it is along this line of something better than deliverance that we must search for the Christian solution of the problem of suffering.

2

ARE CHRISTIANS SPARED?

To get a clue to the Christian solution to this problem, let us look at a passage in which Jesus puts before his followers, in a most vivid picture, the tribulations that would probably come upon them.

Evil is of two kinds: one, which arises from within, from the choices of our wills; that evil we call sin. The other evil comes from without, from our social environment and of the natural universe; that evil we call suffering. It is easy to understand why we should suffer as the result of our inner choices, but why should we suffer when we do not choose? Why should these evils come upon us from without? Jesus tells us very clearly in Luke 21: 8-19, that evils would so come upon us. In this passage, from nine different directions, sufferings come upon us.

There are nine "Blesseds" in the opening words of the Sermon on the Mount, and here in this passage there are nine "Troubles" predicted in the closing words Jesus was having with them. Let us look at these nine avenues of suffering, for in them we see summed up practically all the ways from which sorrow and pain come upon us.

1. Suffering from Confused Counsels in Religion

"Many," he said "shall come in my name, saying, I am he; and, the time is at hand: go ye not after them." There is no doubt that these confused counsels in religion are a deep pain to many. Why aren't things plain and incontrovertible? Religion touches us at our deepest place, and to be uncertain there is to spread uncertainty into the whole of life.

In this age of transition and reconstruction men and women are afflicted in an acute way at this point. Old molds of thought and outlook are being broken up. Life, for many, has lost its old certainties. In the Straits Settlements, one of the schools received an application form for the admission of a pupil filled in by the Chinese father. In the column in which the religion of the parent was to be stated he had written, "Confusion." He meant "Confucian," of course, but he was probably nearer the facts in his misspelling than if he had spelled it correctly. The religion of this age is "Confusion." It was never deeper than at the present time. In one of my meetings, a Hindu chairman rambled on at the close of my address for about as long as I had talked. He alternated in his ramblings between the oldest of orthodoxies and the newest of theories. The crowd was getting restless, but howled with laughter when he capped everything by saying, "I have been studying all religions lately, especially "Confusionism." Everybody could see that he had been studying "Confusionism"!

The religion of this age is "Confusion." It was never deeper than at the present time.

We smile at the brother's statement, but the smile soon fades away and a pain takes its place, for this confusion in our mind eats at our happiness like a canker. No one can be happy with uncertainty at the center. Why has not God made everything clear in this most important place of life, as clear, say, as the multiplication table? Well, suppose he had? Then the mystery would die out of life; adventure of spirit, which is so necessary to character formation, would be absent, and the soul would find no more disposition to pray to a God devoid of beyondness than we have to pray to the multiplication table, however true and clear it may be. No, it is necessary that the deepest things be sufficiently hidden, to develop within us power of discrimination and spiritual insight, by the weighing of alternatives, and by choosing between competing ends the one that seems highest to us. But the process is painful and brings much mental and spiritual suffering.

2. Suffering from Wars and Conflict in Human Society

Jesus says, "You shall hear of wars and rumors of wars." We are members of human society, bound up in a bundle of life that has its conflicts and wars. We may not choose these conflicts; we may loathe and repudiate them, but writhe as we may, we cannot disentangle ourselves from them and their results, in human pain. How few people chose this last war! The ones who really willed it could probably be counted on one's two hands, and yet the millions that suffered and are still suffering from the choice of those few! There was a time when relatively few of the total population suffered when professional armies clashed on a battlefield, but those days of simplicity are gone; life has become so complex and interwoven that a conflict anywhere affects us everywhere. We used to talk about going to war to protect the women and the children and the weaker members of human society. That day is past. We know now that war has lost its power to protect the weak, for no one suffers more in war, as now carried on, than the women and the children. Not merely armies, but whole peoples are involved in war and in its consequent misery.

Certainly, the Christian is not exempt from this particular pain. In fact, he suffers doubly, mentally and spiritually, from the fact that war is an utter denial of all the teaching and spirit of his Lord, and from the fact of actual participation in the physical suffering involved. If here and there a Christian feels that a special providence has saved a loved one in war, it is no answer to the problem of suffering, for how can we explain the fact that equally good Christians did not find themselves or their loved ones spared by a special act of Providence?

3. Suffering from Physical Calamities in Nature such as Earthquakes

"There shall be great earthquakes." Earthquakes strike without asking whether you are good or bad. It is simply not true that earthquakes hit the bad and spare the good. An earthquake in India shook down a mission building and left a brothel standing nearby. In Burma, a severe earthquake shook down everything in the locality, but left a Christian's house standing in the midst of it, and this was considered an act of Providence. But what about those cases where it does not happen in this way? The Christian, providentially spared, answer to this problem leaves us in a road with a dead end, for it doesn't work out in life.

Consider the result if it did work out that way. If it could be proved that the Christian is infallibly spared pain and suffering when it falls on others, the result would be a degradation of Christianity.

The multitudes would flock to our churches and accept Christianity and its protections, as one would take out a fire insurance policy. It would also be the degradation of the Christian, for he would miss that discipline that comes from living in a universe of impartial law. He would be exempted from that struggle with impersonal and impartial forces of nature, out of which alertness and strength of character are formed, and through which he is made mentally and spiritually and physically fit to survive. That exemption would be his elimination. Moreover, his religion would degenerate into magic. He would wear it as we do a talisman. It would become as pernicious as the custom in the Philippines, where the students about to take examinations, bring their pens to the priest to have them blessed in order to assure success in the trial awaiting them. It would weaken his mental and moral fiber. A lady asked me in all seriousness to pray that the ticket, which she had taken on the Derby Sweepstakes, might be the winning one; if I did, she added, and the ticket won, she would "divide half the amount with the church." I replied that I would pray that she might get a new conception of religion in general and of Christianity in particular.

Christianity is not a magical, but a moral revelation, and the end is the production of moral character, and not the saving of its devotees in particular situations from the operation of the laws of physical phenomena. The head of a school who enrolled his child in his own school but exempted the child from the operations of the disciplines and penalties of the school, would do himself, the child, and the school a distinct and serious harm.

Jesus told us that we would suffer from earthquakes.

And we do.

4. Suffering from Physical Sicknesses and Infirmities

"There shall be…pestilences." There are those who say that God always undertakes to spare his children from pestilences and to heal their sicknesses, and that when this result is not obtained, it is a lack of faith that is responsible. That God does heal diseases by his direct touch upon men and women, I have not the slightest doubt. Has not my own wonderful physical health, beginning fifteen years ago, been the direct result of a touch that I received at that time? To deny this would be to deny my very life. But that God promises always to heal all disease, and that an absence of such healing is a sign of a lack of faith I seriously question. Some of the greatest saints have been smitten with pestilence and the finest of the earth have languished on beds of pain.

> *Christianity is not a magical, but a moral revelation, and the end is the production of moral character, and not the saving of its devotees in particular situations from the operation of the laws of physical phenomena.*

A young consecrated mission doctor in Mukden, beloved of all, fighting almost alone a scourge of pneumonic plague, was stricken in the midst of it and died, when he was seemingly most needed. Howard Walter, a rare, saintly spirit, with brilliant gifts and just coming to his period of greatest usefulness, was stricken in his young manhood and died of influenza just when India needed him most. The blow shattered the health of his wife, and scattered the children among relatives, a home broken up. And yet, who were seemingly more qualified to set up a model home than those two rare souls? The cholera germs that killed John Forman, the saint, did not stop because they were attacking consecrated flesh.

I know that the ancient Jewish writers seemed to hold out something different when they said,

A thousand shall fall at thy side,
And ten thousand at thy right hand;
But it shall not come nigh thee.
Only with thine eyes shalt thou behold
And see the reward of the wicked. . .
There shall no evil befall thee,
Neither shall any plague come nigh thy tent...
With long life will I satisfy him.

If you spiritualize this, it can be used; but if it is to be taken literally, then it raises questions. The New Testament does not teach this. Nor does life teach it. It is the insistence upon the literal fulfillment of such promises, as the above and the conflict it raises, with the daily facts around one, that stuns and shatters the faith of many. It simply does not work out that no plague comes near the dwelling of the righteous and that they are invariably satisfied with long life. It is quite true that righteousness does tend to saner and healthier and longer living. A life lived in the Christian way fits the facts of the universe better, makes a man happier, and therefore on the whole gives longer life. But the exceptions to this are so many that we cannot expect the solution of the problem of suffering to consist in being spared from plague, and being satisfied with invariably long life. It raises more problems than it settles.

5. Suffering from Economic Distress

"There shall be famines." The economic distress upon the world at the present time brings home this problem in an acute form. An unemployed man breaks my heart. What is the answer to this form of suffering? Are the good, prosperous, and the bad, economically pinched? It is true that in the long run, the good will probably be better off economically, for the universe stands behind righteousness and stands against evil. The universe is not built for the success of a lie, whether it be a lie in lips, or a lie in merchandise. But, it is difficult to prove, that this prosperity works out always for the individual here and now.

The book of Job takes up this problem of suffering, and ends the whole drama by saying that Job got back just double what he had before his losses, and that he lived to a ripe old age. Again, if you spiritualize this and make it include heaven within the scope of its operation, we may use it; but if you insist upon its literally working out in life that way, then we are up against insuperable difficulties. The New Testament does not give this for an answer. It does not promise here and now, a ripe old age and a double return for all losses in this life.

It is true that there is one passage in the New Testament which seems to teach this: "There is no man that hath left house or brethren, or sisters, or mother, or father, or children, or lands, for my sake, and for the gospel's sake, but he shall receive a hundredfold now in this time, houses, and brethren, and sisters, and mothers, and children, and lands, with persecutions; and in the world to come, eternal life" (Mark 10. 29, 30). But this can scarcely be taken literally in the case of the "houses" and "lands," any more than it can be taken in the case of the "mothers," where it is obviously impossible to have "mothers" a hundredfold. Unquestionably, it must be taken with a metaphorical meaning, namely, that when we belong to Christ, we own nothing and yet everything is ours, all women our sisters, all men our brothers, all mothers our mothers, all houses and lands our houses and lands, we are children of the Father; he owns all, and we use the inheritance while owning nothing. But note that the account adds, "with persecutions," to remind them that what he was offering was not a way of material gain or pleasure, but an inner attitude of life, that owning nothing, possessed everything, and exulted even in persecutions.

Jesus had nothing to divide at his death except his seamless robe. Peter was compelled to say at the Beautiful Gate, "Silver and gold have I none." Paul died penniless.

It is true that Jesus said that if you "seek first the kingdom of God, all these things shall be added unto you"; but the "all things" that were to be added were "food" and "clothing." Life has now become so complex, wants have been so multiplied and made into necessities, that for most of us to get only food and clothing would be akin to "famine."

The Christian is not guaranteed against economic loss, nor will he be repaid double for losses incurred in this life. There is no book of Job in the New Testament. It has its own distinctive answer to the problem of suffering.

6. Suffering from one's Own Fellow Men and Women

"They shall lay their hands on you and persecute you." Society demands conformity. If you fall below its standards, it will punish you; and if you rise above its standards, it will persecute you. The Christian is the creation of a new type of being, as different from the ordinary man, as the ordinary man is from the animal. In the language of biology, he is "a variation" upward. He is the embryonic swan, but in the meantime to human society, he is the "ugly duckling" and is "picked on" accordingly. When I announced to my companion in the law library, where I was working, that I had been converted the night before, he promptly replied in a tone of scorn, "I'll knock that out of you in two weeks." He, representing human society, had the sure instinct that I was getting out of hand, so he immediately began to "lay hands" on me.

Of course, it is dangerous to get "the persecution complex," for many Christians think they are wearing martyrs' crowns, when they are only wearing fools' caps. Self-pity is the most pitiable of all pities. A whining attitude is a weakening attitude. The Christian must have nothing to do with it. He follows a Master who, while on his way to a cross, said to the women weeping for and pitying him, "Weep not for me." The Christian, if he is to keep his self-respect, must say the same.

While making allowance for the possibility of a persecution complex, there still remains the fact that Christianity is an affront to things as they are, and the Christian who departs from the accepted order of things, will be looked on as "odd," and will often have to pay the penalty for the departure. "They will lay hands on you," as my companion did to me in the law library.

7. Suffering from Religious and Secular Authorities

"They shall persecute you, delivering you up to the synagogues and prisons." Here are two types of trouble represented by the word "synagogue" and by the word "prison," one religious and the other secular. There is a sting in that word "synagogue." We would have expected him to use the word "temple," for the temple was the more hardened institution standing for the rule of the priest. But the synagogue represented a more or less lay institution, more congregational and freer. At the heart of the temple was the stone now found in a Constantinople museum with the inscription on it, "Let no foreigner enter within the screen and enclosure around the Holy Place. Whosoever is taken so doing will himself, be the cause that death overtakes him." There was no such sentiment in the synagogue. It stood for freedom. But an institution standing initially for freedom, now becomes an instrument of persecution. It is the old story, the history of almost all religious denominations. They begin with revolt and end with stifling all revolt from themselves. This is the depravity of institutions; in the beginning they are given to express life, they end, however, in throttling that very life. They therefore need recurrent criticism, constant readjustment, and a perpetual realignment with life and progress. But the one who attempts this realignment will find exactly what Jesus found, when he announced his program of freedom in the synagogue at Nazareth. "They were all filled with wrath in the synagogue, and they rose up, . . . and led him unto the brow of the hill where their city was built, that they could cast him down headlong." The result of any departure may be persecution, as open as the casting down from the brow of the hill, or it may be as subtle as the arching of the brows of our companions in the synagogue; in either case the heart has closed and we are on the

> *Freedom has turned into freedom to persecute—the light has turned into darkness, and how great is that darkness!*

outside. Freedom has turned into freedom to persecute—the light has turned into darkness, and how great is that darkness!

Or the suffering may come from authority in secular affairs: "bringing you before kings and governors." The state demands the right to be supreme, and even to coerce the conscience of the individual. Two students in China went to a magistrate to protest against the arrest of some of their companions for marching in a patriotic procession. By their insistence, they offended the dignity of the magistrate. He demanded that they apologize on bended knees or else be shot. One of them, to save himself, made the apology. The other refused, saying that the time had gone by, when they bent the knee to anyone. The magistrate ordered him to be shot in the feet; but standing on wounded feet, he still protested against the injustice done to his comrades. The magistrate ordered that he be shot through the abdomen. They did so, but he still protested. Then the soldiers were ordered to shoot him through the neck, and as the student fell over, his last words were the reiterated protest. Most of us have no such courage before insolent might. We bend the knee and conform to unjust authority. The amount of suffering which innocent and righteous people have undergone through unrighteous authority, is incalculable.

8. Suffering through the Home Life

"You shall be delivered up even by parents, and brethren, and kinsfolk, and friends." These words refer to the specific betrayal of the follower of Christ by those in his own home. This kind of suffering is real in the early stages of the acceptance of Christ in a non-Christian land. I have looked into hundreds of faces of young people and seen them tortured, with the pain of finding themselves cast out of the home circle, because of their new spiritual allegiance to Christ! Only the inward urge of the Spirit could carry them through this pain.

This particular kind of suffering in the home is very real, but not as widespread as the kind that arises from the incompatibilities and the daily irritations of unhappy homes. Through loyalty to the other members of the family, the face wears a smile before the world, while the cross of a constant irritation presses upon the sensitive spirit. But it is worn in silence.

When I spoke to Dr. Hu Shih, the father of the Renaissance Movement in China, about Christ fulfilling the best in Chinese culture and life, mentioning the home life of the Chinese as a thing to be preserved, he replied: "But which of our homes are happy? None!" An overstatement, of course, but think of the possibility of unhappiness of the most intimate kind, in the homes of four hundred million people. Then, spread that through the rest of the world in more or less varying degrees, and you have an amount of unhappiness that is enough to wring the heart of a statue. Suffering in the home has been increased by the shadow of unemployment. The sting of not being able to support wife and child who are dependent upon the father, eats like acid into sensitive natures.

It is not true that the Christian is always spared the pain that can come through home life. Sometimes the incompatibilities between husband and wife are heightened, because of the difference in ideals and allegiance. It is true that because the Christian lives more in harmony with the moral universe, many are saved from those hurts that come from being out of harmony with moral law. But there are other sources of suffering in the home, from which neither partner appears to escape.

9. Suffering from the Fact of Being Associated with Christ

"You shall be hated of all men for my name's sake." Simeon, the aged saint, saw that Christ would be "a sign" that would "be spoken against." He was right. Christ has been. For by his uncompromising attitude, he puts things in such a way that we have either to crucify our lusts, or crucify him. Someone has said that if Christ came to Congress, he would first be popular, then puzzling, and then persecuted. We either passionately love him or passionately hate him. Of course, we can take neutral attitudes toward him, but only if we stay in the dim distance from him. Get close to him, and the soul either stiffens in opposition or melts in surrender. The Christian partakes of that same uncompromising quality.

Christ on his cross disturbed "the feast" at Jerusalem. The Jewish leaders asked that he be taken down from the cross, for his presence upset their feast. The Christian upsets the trivialities of men by the grandeur of his purposes, and disturbs their feasts by his sacrificial spirit. The Christian is, therefore, not a popular hero. No monument has ever been set up in any city of the world for the world's most heroic figure, "The Christian." To military heroes? Yes. But not to the Christian. A statue set up in Princeton University campus, entitled "The Christian Student," evoked an agitation for its removal. It was too much of a judgment seat.

Secretly in our heart of hearts we may admire the Christian ideal, but superficially we fight it until we surrender. Then it becomes to us all in all. The words of Jesus are literally a fact, "Woe unto you, when all men shall speak well of you," for if they do, then you are accommodating yourself to all men, including their sins.

Christ being what he is, and the Christian being what she should be, is bound to know suffering as the result of following that Christ.

Here, then, we see that suffering comes upon us from nine different avenues: From the mental and spiritual confusions in regard to the deepest things of life; from the association with society, which becomes involved in wars; from the fact of physical calamities, coming from the rampant powers of nature, such as earthquake, fire, flood, and storm; from pestilences that creep silently into our foods, into the air that we breathe, and into the polluting touch of our fellow men; from economic distress; from the fact that society lays hands on us, because of our departing from its spirit and standards; from the oppression that comes from religious and secular authorities; from the incompatibilities of the home; and from association with the Man whose symbol is a cross. Surely, there is no promise to the good man, that he will be granted an immunity and protection from the sufferings that fall on others.

> *What answer can we give to this undoubted fact of unmerited suffering? In giving that answer we must walk softly...*

To complete the picture, we must add to the above nine special ways that trouble comes, the fact that death steals into our homes and, whether they be homes of goodness or of evil, takes away our dearest, sometimes at the very height of their power and usefulness. Death is the universal fact. I glanced up from the writing of that sentence and my eyes fell upon these lines in a letter on my desk, "When my husband passed beyond, my one desire was to get away from the world, to find some corner to be alone in with my hurt." The woman who wrote those lines is one of the noblest and gentlest, the very epitome of all that is finest and most beautiful in womanhood, and yet she was left alone to face the world with six small children.

In sketching the face of humanity, I trust that I have not drawn the lines of suffering too deeply. There are other sides, of course, but that there is this side cannot be escaped. What answer can we give to this undoubted fact of unmerited suffering? In giving that answer we must walk softly, lest in bungling, we add to suffering, the disappointment and disillusionment that come from following ways that "keep the word of promise to our ears, and break it to our hope." We must tread this ground with a prayer upon our lips.

3

VARIOUS WAYS OF FACING HUMAN SUFFERING

What are the various answers given to this problem of suffering? In looking across the world of human thought, one is struck with the variety of answers. Most all of them are sincere, for at this point men lay aside the spirit of trifling cleverness. We may not agree with the answers given, but we are struck with the evident sincerity of them.

1. Remake the World with the Possibility of Suffering Left Out

Omar Khayyam, the Persian poet, looked upon the world with its misery and pain, and in his fierce reaction against it proposed:

"To grasp this sorry Scheme of Things entire,
. . . shatter it to bits, and then
Remold it nearer to the Heart's desire!"

In the "Rubaiyat," he presents perhaps the most thoroughgoing reaction against the world and also the most thoroughgoing remedy for the problem of suffering, he would *remake the world with the possibility of suffering left out of it.* This may be "the heart's desire" of many of us at times of peculiar perplexity and pain, and yet it remains only a heart's desire, for we know that we have no power to put it into effect; nor does our mind in its most thoughtful moments accept the thought of a world with the possibility of pain left out. In our mind of minds, we know that the end of life is character and not happiness, and that happiness can only be a by-product of that character, and without the possibility of pain we are not sure that character could be attained.

We must accept the world as it is, and try to find the solution of the problem of suffering, not through fantasies of smashing universes, but through the facts as they are. We must start with things as they are, there must be no dodging of issues, there must be no illusions. For every exaggeration ends in prostration, whose only issue is death.

2. Accepting the Fact of Suffering, and Trying to Meet It, by Always Anticipating It

This is *the opposite of the* first answer to the problem of suffering. This method of accepting the fact of suffering, and trying to meet it, by always anticipating it, is the type of mentality tries to cheat the jinx, by always expecting it. It says to itself: "I knew it would come. I was not caught unawares, for I hold everything, expecting it to be snatched from my hands." This is the attitude of disillusioned cynicism. It gets what happiness it can, out of the fact that it knew beforehand, that there was no happiness. This perspective is a rather thin diet, it is true, but many who take it are able to point to their own anemic lives as proof of the truth of their contention that there is no real happiness. But it hardly solves the problem of suffering, it only illustrates it.

3. The Attitude of Self-pity

Some people meet the problem of suffering by feeling sorry for themselves and get pleasure out of feeling sorry for themselves. Many exaggerate their troubles in order to enlarge the possibility of self-pity. There is a touch of this in the fact that almost every man thinks his troubles to be the greatest.

I was once on my way home after a long tour, and naturally anxious to get home. But I missed five different train connections at five different junctions, one after the other, until I wondered if the railways were entering into a conspiracy to keep me away from home, for none of these misses were due to any fault of mine. I remember in my perplexity praying the prayer, "Lord, is there anything you want to teach me through these delays? Please teach it to me and let me get home!" I was twenty-four hours late when I arrived at the station in Sitapur on a midnight train. At that time of the year, February, we do not have rain but once in a blue moon, but just as I arrived at the station a terrific thunderstorm broke. I was on a little unprotected native cart, an *ekka*, and it took us two hours to get the two miles from the station to my house. I was soaked to the skin and it was cold. But as I came into the Mission compound, I saw a light on the veranda. How welcome it seemed! The missionary who was living in the same house met me, as I jumped from the ekka and ran on the veranda, soaked and feeling very sorry for myself after the escapade of misses, culminating in this! I expected some expression of sympathy and pity, but his first words were, "I haven't slept a wink all night." I lay back and laughed. He was astonished at my laughter, but I saw my lesson. Every man thinks his troubles are the greatest! He was concentrating on his own sleeplessness, and I was concentrated on my combination of troubles, and each was pitying himself.

In this case it was laughable, but very often it becomes a serious malady. Missionaries are peculiarly liable to it. It can often be seen protruding itself, as we recount how many burdens are on us, how bad the climate is, and how weary we are! But to meet trouble with self-pity, is only to create a pitiable and pitiful self.

4. The Attitude of Stoicism

This is the attitude of accepting the fact of suffering, and inwardly steeling oneself against it. An Indian tribe in South America begins early to instill this attitude into its young, for as soon as a child is born the father greets it with these words: "You are born into a world of trouble. Shut your mouth, be quiet and bear it." The stoical Indian is the product of this early hardening.

In more elegant language, but breathing the same spirit, are the words, "My head might be bloody, but it will be unbowed, under the bludgeoning of Chance." Many repeat this sentiment to themselves to harden themselves inwardly, against the knocks of life.

There is a touch of the lofty spirit in the words of Abigail Cresson, and they compel our admiration:

"Though I am beaten
Nobody shall know.
I'll wear defeat proudly;
I shall go

"About my business
As I did before.
Only when I have safely
Closed the door

"Against friends and the rest
Shall I be free
To bow my head
Where there is none to see.

"Tonight, I will shed my tears;
Tomorrow when I talk with you
I will be joyous again.

"Though I am beaten
Nobody shall guess, For I will walk
As though I knew success."

These tender lines of a noble-spirited girl find enlarged and somber echo, in the vast and splendid pessimism of German philosopher and historian Oswald Spengler, who after describing the decay of all things, including man and his civilization, ends in these words:

> *Time does not suffer itself to be halted; there is no question of prudent retreat or wise renunciation.*

> Time does not suffer itself to be halted; there is no question of prudent retreat or wise renunciation. Only dreamers believe there is a way out. Optimism is cowardice. We are born into this time and must bravely follow the path to the predestined end. There is no other way. Our duty is to hold on to the lost position, without hope, without rescue, like that Roman soldier whose bones were found in Pompeii, who during the eruption of Vesuvius, died at his post because they forgot to relieve him. That

is greatness. That is what it means to be a thoroughbred. The honorable end is the one thing that cannot be taken from man.

Bertrand Russell puts the same attitude in smaller compass when he says that, "the fairest achievements of man are destined to be destroyed, at last by the trampling march of unconscious power," and that therefore, the best that we can do is to hold "an unyielding despair." In the words of another humanist Joseph Krutch: "Ours is a lost cause, and there is no place for us in the natural universe; but for all that, we are not sorry to be human. We would rather die as men than live as animals." Spengler says, again, that "we human beings of the twentieth-century go downhill, seeing." This somber procession which he describes may go downhill, "seeing," but, it is hardly seeing a way out. The road leads to deepening shadows and final night, and the only light is the flickering spirit of man, momentarily flaring up in protest, just before it goes out eternally.

A very brilliant lecturer on psychology said to me with tears in her eyes, "There is no meaning anywhere, and all I can hope for is that my spirit will not break, and that I will go down in the end, with my head up, as befits one with my breeding."

This attitude and spirit and final end are about as far removed from the Christian solution as can be.

5. The Attitude of Buddha

The gentle Buddha sat under the Bo tree at Gaya, and in his deep meditations discovered the four sacred truths: Suffering, the cause of suffering, the destruction of suffering, and the way to the destruction of suffering. He summed it all up in the startling conclusion: "Existence and suffering are one." He went further than saying, that there is suffering in existence, he said that suffering and existence are fundamentally and inextricably one. From this basis, he began to work his way out toward a solution. The way was this: The thing that keeps us going in the round of rebirths is desire, for out of desire deeds spring, and deeds keep up the necessity of the weary round of birth and rebirth, to get the fruit of those deeds. As long as there are deeds, there will be the result of those deeds, this is the law of Karma. The law of Karma necessitates the coming back to birth, to work out the overplus of reward or punishment. Buddha then propounded the obvious proposition,—that to deal with this whole evil, we must go back beyond the deed, to the desire. We must cut out the root of desire, even for existence itself. Then, one will get out into that passionless, actionless state of Nirvana. This state is the dissolution of personality, as we now know it. If it isn't the cessation of being, it is at least the cessation of becoming. It is the state literally of, "the snuffed-out candle." In this state, one has passed beyond all pain, all suffering, and in fact, all everything. For there is no "one" to suffer.

Until the follower of the Buddha attains that, he is to be compassionate to all men and creatures, for they are all bound up in the Weary Round of Suffering. But the enlightened one, is to manifest this spirit of compassion, in a spirit of disinterested, disillusioned aloofness. He does these things as one who does not do them. Desire has been cut, and action will go on, as a wheel once turned will continue to turn, even after the force applied has been removed, but gradually it will cease to turn and come to rest. So, the enlightened one who has cut the root of all desire, will go on with his deeds of compassion, until the final and everlasting rest in Nirvana.

There is something lofty and grand about Buddha, even when one must fundamentally differ with him, regarding his basic principle that existence and evil are one. For we must differ with him in this. Jesus said that there is evil in existence, but get the evil out, and you will find that existence is fundamentally good, "I am come that they might have life, and that they might have it more abundantly." Buddha would reduce life to that of the vegetable and call it victory. Buddha would counsel us to get rid of the personality in order to get rid of the suffering bound up with personality, in other words, to get rid of our headache by cutting off our head. It is a remedy, but at too big a price.

And yet Buddha was right in diagnosing our difficulty as "desire." It is the desires of men reaching out to this thing and that thing that leaves them disillusioned, pained, and in suffering. We seem to be infinite beings trying to find satisfaction with finite things. The result is suffering! Yes, Buddha was right in finding the root of our difficulty to be in desire, but he was wrong in his remedy. He would try to get rid of all desire, when the fact is that there is no possible way to get rid of one desire except to replace it by a higher desire. One does not get rid of desire by its suppression, but by its expression in a higher form. Love fastened upon the flesh, degenerates into lust and is degrading, but fastened upon a personality like Christ, rises into a higher form and is redeeming. In the one case it brings suffering, and in the other case it brings the cure of suffering. The unsatisfied desire is therefore removed, not by its extinction, but

"Love fastened upon the flesh, degenerates into lust and is degrading, but fastened upon a personality like Christ, rises into a higher form and is redeeming."

through its satisfaction. The love of the lower is cast out by the love of the higher. Buddha caught glimpses of the truth, but the final truth evaded him, for he saw no One, who was worthy of fastening our love upon, —-the gods spoiled God for him. Since the heavens were blank, earth too, was blank, life was blank, and the only possible end is the state of "the snuffed-out candle." When you lose God, as Buddha seems to have done, then life itself goes to pieces. The arches crash, for there is no keystone to hold them together. You cannot believe long in man unless you believe in something more than man, you cannot believe in life unless you believe in Life.

There is an attitude akin to Buddhism in the order of Christian nuns whose one greeting to each other is the words, "Sisters, we are born to die." There is also an order of monks who are called "The Grave Diggers" from the fact that each day they dig a shovelful of earth from the hole that will one day be their own grave, thus reminding themselves daily that the end is death. This practice is more Buddhist than Christian.

6. The Hindu Attitude toward Suffering

The Hindu holds an attitude akin to that of the Buddhist, for he too, views the injustices and inequalities of life, and *posits a previous birth, from which all these sufferings and inequalities come.* The sufferings, which we think come from our environment and from our fellow men, are not really from them, the Hindu says, for they are from our own choices in a previous birth. All suffering has its antecedent sin, somewhere. As a calf will find its mother among a thousand cows, so your deeds will find you amid a thousand births. All suffering, therefore, is just. "Jesus must have been a terrible sinner in a previous birth, for he was such a sufferer in this one," said a Hindu to me one day. From his premises, he was logically right. "Why do we help the sick in the hospitals, by doing so, are we not interfering with the law of Karma, which is making them suffer as a result of their previous deeds?" asked another Hindu. He was right from his standpoint. Two students were living above low-caste people in the rooms below. The students thoughtlessly threw their garbage down on the outcastes beneath. One student's conscience was aroused, and he suggested that they desist with throwing trash on others. "But," said the Hindu, "these people are low caste, because of sin in a previous birth, and they could not suffer from us unless they deserved it." Karma had justified their sufferings, for, according to it, everything that is, is just.

Of course, many things are softening and modifying this outlook, so that the Hindu is usually better in his attitudes toward suffering than the doctrine would suggest, but that it is there, and that, it seems to me, is the real root of the tendency for every reform in Hinduism to be halting.

Now, the Hindu of the Vedantic school, and this is the really dominant philosophy in India, points the way out of suffering by positing our identity with the Divine. "*Tat twam asi*"— "Thou art That," is the supreme affirmation of Vedantism, and when the devotee learns to reply in very truth, *"Aham Brahmasmi"* – "I am Brahma," —then he is released from all bonds, all sufferings, he is merged into the Divine, or rather, he recognizes his essential oneness with the Divine. For the reason he seems separate is because of *Avidya*, ignorance, which brings *Maya*, illusion, the illusion of the reality of the world and of our separateness from the Divine. Since Brahma in its highest state, the Nirguna, which means without relationships, without bonds, without deeds, is that state of pure being, the devotee is to cease all deeds, good or bad, concentrate his attention between his eyebrows in his dreamy silence, and thus realizing his unity with Brahma, pass out into It. I say, "It," for Brahma is impersonal.

While the devotee is in the process of realizing this, he may do good deeds, provided he does them *"nishkarma,"* without desire for fruit or reward. He is to do them in a detached, aloof way. He has no attachment to anything, he belongs to the Detached, the Great Aloof. He steps out of the wheel of rebirth, and finally enters into Brahma, who is *"sat, chit, ananda,"* being, intelligence, bliss. His personality is lost at last, in the ocean of Being, and with it there is, of course, a cessation of all sorrow, all suffering.

The Hindu, therefore, lays the basis of suffering in a twofold fact, the fact of rebirth, which accounts for the inequalities and sufferings of this life, and the fact of the sense of separateness from the Divine.

In examining this answer to the problem of suffering, are we confined to the hypothesis of a previous birth, to account for the inequalities and sufferings of this life? Is there any other way to account for inequalities and sufferings?

Before we enter into a discussion of this, let us plainly state that there is a deep and abiding truth in the law of Karma. We do reap what we sow. This is a universe of moral law. We shall discuss this more thoroughly later. Rebirth is a hypothesis, added to the law of Karma, to explain the inequalities of life. It is a corollary, but no necessary part, of the doctrine of Karma. One may believe in Karma and not accept the hypothesis of rebirth. For it is only a hypothesis, incapable either of proof or of disproof. One may see evidence sufficient to accept the hypothesis, or may deem it insufficient and reject it. But there is no proof. Can we account for inequalities on another basis, and one which is more satisfactory than that offered by rebirth? I think we can.

There are three distinct streams of influence which make for inequalities. One is the innate heredity, our genetics. Parents differ and pass on different qualities to their children. The influence of heredity may skip back to a grandparent or great-grandparent, but whether immediate or remote, it is a powerful influence in the producing of differences that may sometimes seem to be inequalities. But genetics does not account for all inequalities.

There is another stream of inequalities coming from the social heredity. By the social heredity, we mean the sum total of influences that play upon the child from without, the environmental, the social, the moral, the religious, the climatic, and the political. Society is organized in favor of some and against others. A child born in an outcaste home in India, is subjected to a set of influences that largely determine what kind of a man or woman he or she will be. But take that child from birth out of its social heredity, and subject it to a new set of social influences, and one can practically make a new being out of it. Many things which we think are inherent, are only environmentally and socially conditioned. The social heredity has a powerful influence in producing inequalities in life. But it is not all-conclusive, as the mechanistic psychologists would claim.

There is a third stream making for inequalities, namely, a person's own choices. Within the framework of one's innate and social heredities, there is sufficient freedom for moral choice. This freedom is sufficient for one to determine his own character by his own choices. As Johnson said, "We are free, and we know it, and that is an end of it." These choices may cancel or congeal many of the tendencies that come from the innate (genetic) and the social heredities.

These three streams, the innate and the social heredities and a person's own choices are sufficient to account for the inequalities of life. No one of the three taken by itself, can account for these inequalities, but taken together they can, and do. And let us be reminded that these factors are not hypotheses, but laws actually at work. We are more and more discovering what sort of 'laws' belongs to each. If the Hindu thinkers had known of the laws of heredity, they would not have been forced into the hypothesis of a previous birth to explain inequalities.

Moreover, the theory of rebirth can hardly be called a very just, or adequate system of rewards and punishments. There is no memory brought over from one birth to another, and therefore to punish one without connecting fault and punishment by the link of memory, can hardly be called a system worthy of the justice of the universe. It is no answer to say that some people do remember their previous births, for this assertion too is incapable of proof; and if it could be proved, it would still be without universal application, for only one or two out of millions of persons ever even claim to remember a previous birth. It would be like punishing a boy of eighteen for faults done in childhood, of which he has no memory, and concerning which the punisher refuses to enlighten him.

These three streams account for the inequalities, but they do not justify them, for we are only accountable for the stream of our own choices. We cannot choose our parents, nor can we choose the social heredity in which we are born. Of course, we are responsible for the passing on of innate heredities when we become parents, and for the passing on of the social heredities when we become members of society and put our stamp of approval on any resulting inequality, producing social systems. But the center of our responsibility rests on our own choices. The New Testament recognizes this and announces the idea of differing degrees of responsibility. It says in essence: "To whom little has been given, little shall be required; to whom much has been given much shall be required." To whom little has been given in these innate and social heredities, little shall be required at the place of responsibility of choice; to whom much has been given in these heredities, much shall be required. A varying standard of responsibility will right the inequalities. These three streams account for them, and a varying standard of judgment will right them.

But while that answer is true as far as it goes, it lacks the full content of the Christian answer. It lacks a final touch. That final touch is the part that God takes in receiving these inequalities and injustices upon his own heart, to let them break it upon a cross. Here the universe becomes not only just, but redemptive. We must return to this later.

We must now look at the Hindu solution of suffering, by considering oneself part of the Divine. The Hindu says that since we are God, there can be no sin, no suffering. Salvation is to be by *Gyana*, knowledge. This is not knowledge in general, but the specific knowledge that one is God. In that knowledge, passes away all thought of sin and suffering as part of *Maya,* illusion. This is obviously very different from Buddha's conception. Buddha said that existence is suffering, and the Vedanta says that there is no suffering at all.

How does this way work? It is certainly a sublime affirmation to wave out of existence with one glorious gesture, all the pain and suffering there is. But one has the feeling that it is an attitude that can scarcely stand the shock of the facts of life. It may lift one up while he is drunk on the wine of this idea, but there is the inevitable reaction, the inevitable "morning after the night before." Buddhism with its pessimism about all being suffering, is the morning after the night before of Vedantism, with its strained affirmations of there being no suffering.

In one of our Round Table Conferences a Swami told of what religion meant to him in experience: "I am the Divine. I am the Mother of all. All people are my sons and daughters. I have no sickness, no sorrow, no pain." After this remarkable statement he caused us inwardly to collapse by saying, "Now you must excuse me for I must go and worship Hannuman." Hannuman is "the monkey god" of mythological Hinduism. Whenever you try to lift yourself up by an overstrained statement such as the above, it is bound to be followed by some such descent as the Hannuman illustration. Polytheism always coexists with pantheism. India, holding to that doctrine, that all is the Divine and hence there is no suffering, has had the Nemesis come on her of being the land of the greatest suffering in the world. Instead of acknowledging the suffering and facing it and getting rid of it, Vedanta waves it out of existence and pays the penalty. For we repeat, all exaggeration ends in prostration whose only issue is death.

Instead of acknowledging the suffering and facing it and getting rid of it, Vedanta waves it out of existence and pays the penalty.

There is a nobler method tried by the Hindus in acknowledging the existence of suffering, that of maintaining an attitude of indifference. The ideal is the poised man who withdraws within himself, and is indifferent to praise or blame, heat or cold, pleasure or pain. This is noble, but it falls far short of the active Christian way of love. In the early Christian centuries, they tried to Christianize the term and conception of the Greek ideal of "Apathy." However, it could not be done. The active principle of love within Christianity prevented this negation. The Christian method of life is not and cannot be withdrawal from life.

7. The Muslim Attitude toward Suffering is that all that Happens is God's will.

This is perhaps simpler than any other attitude. The Muslim is impressed with the sovereignty of God. All that happens is God's will. God has predetermined and predestined all that happens. The good and the evil that come upon us are alike his will. The attitude of the faithful is to submit to that will. Islam literally means submission to the will of God. The Muslim view of suffering, therefore, is to accept it as the will of God and submit to it.

There is no doubt that this attitude has produced "the patient East," patient, yes, but not progressive. The East is now demanding progressive life, so that Indians more and more rebel against this acceptance of everything as the will of God. They see it as an incubus upon the soul of a nation. A friend of mine, a Swami, was talking to a rich landowner and taking him to task about his oppression of his tenants, but the landowner countered every embarrassing query by unctuously saying, "It is the will of God for them." The Swami lost patience, pulled off his shoe, and struck the rich landowner, saying, "Then this is the will of God for you!" The landowner was furious at such an indignity, the worst that can be given to an Indian, and threatened court proceedings against the Swami. But, upon further reflection, he changed his mind and decided to dedicate a temple to the courageous Swami, and did! India is less and less ascribing things to the sovereign will of God. Her temples will more and more be dedicated to those who show a righteous wrath against the ones who cover exploitation with piety, and hide their predatory wills under "the will of God" cloak. To ascribe all suffering to the will of God is the new blasphemy.

Islam, great and noble in many ways, has nevertheless sterilized the life of vast portions of the East, because its acceptance of inequalities and sufferings as the will of God lays a paralyzing hand on any civilization that adopts it. It is an opiate.

8. The Jewish Attitude toward Suffering Links the Absence of Suffering to Righteousness

In our discussion in a previous chapter we noted in passing that the Jewish mind felt that God would look "with favor upon his people," would "save them out of all their troubles," would let no "plague" come nigh the dwelling of the righteous, would give the righteous double for all his losses, and would satisfy him with long life and prosperity. It is true that some of the prophets, Habakkuk, for example, struck a deeper note in the glorious words:

"For though the fig tree shall not blossom,
Neither shall fruit be in the vines,
The labor of the olive shall fail,
And the fields shall yield no meat;
The flock shall be cut off from the fold,
And there shall be no herd in the stalls:
Yet I will rejoice in the Lord,
I will joy in the God of my salvation."

Isaiah went deeper still, when he depicted the Suffering Servant: "By oppression and judgment he was taken away; and as for his generation, who among them considered that he was cut off out of the land of the living? . . . They made his grave with the wicked, and with the rich in his death, although he had done no violence, neither was any deceit in his mouth. Yet it pleased the Lord to bruise him." Here was another note, deeper and cutting straight across the surface note of expectation that the righteous would be prosperous and live long, and see only with his eyes the troubles that would fall on others.

The Jewish nation as a whole never responded to that deeper note, and when Jesus sounded it in his own life and teaching and outlook, they rejected it, taunting him at the end as he hung on his cross, that God would show that he was pleased with Jesus, only if God saved him from the cross. God did not intervene, so they felt doubly sure as they went home from the cross, that they had been dealing with a "deceiver."

Islam has inherited this same attitude about Jesus. They believe him to be a prophet, but they cannot bear to see the prophet of God end ignominiously upon a cross, so they teach that Jesus was miraculously saved from the cross, taken triumphantly to heaven and another crucified in his stead.

This Semitic line of thought has passed over into Christendom in spite of the cross. The confusion within Christendom concerning suffering arises from the attempt to reconcile these two conflicting elements. When we as faithful Christians are not spared troubles, our faith is deeply shocked, for we have back in our minds these Jewish promises that we would be spared. These promises do not square with life, so the foundations of our faith give way. We are unmindful of the fact that the New Testament holds out no such promises, but has a different attitude and method for the facing of suffering. We need not anticipate just now what that attitude is, except to call attention to the altogether different note which sounds in the words of Jesus, "In the world you shall have tribulation: but be of good cheer; I have overcome the world."

9. The Christian-Science Method of Dealing with Suffering and Pain Denies the Reality of Sin, Suffering and Death as Unreal

This method may be summed up in brief as follows: All is the Eternal Mind and is the Sole Reality; we are a part of that Mind; that Mind can have nothing evil in it; therefore all is good; there is no such thing as sin and suffering and death; these things belong to the realm of the unreal and exist only in mortal mind; realize your identity with the Eternal Mind and all sin and suffering and death pass away as unrealities.

> *Many sicknesses are mentally conditioned and feed upon depressed mental states.*

Many have doubtless been helped by this method, for there is running through it a strain of wonderful optimism. To many who have been centered on themselves and their troubles, it has come with a sense of healing relief. Many sicknesses are mentally conditioned and feed upon depressed mental states. Christian Science sounds a note of glorious optimism to these mental sufferers, telling them to lift up their heads, to look out of themselves, to get a vision of the Ultimate Good in which there is no pain or suffering. I have no doubt that this changed attitude from pessimism to optimism heals many.

As the reader has doubtlessly noticed, there is a very strong likeness between Christian Science and Hindu Vedantism. Both teach that there is one Sole Reality, Vedanta calls it *Atma*, or Spirit; Christian Science calls it Mind; both teach that we are identified with that Spirit or Mind, that matter, pain, suffering, sin, and death belong to that world of *Maya*, or illusion; both teach that we are redeemed from all sin and suffering by knowledge, knowledge of our identity with the Eternal Mind or Spirit.

Both Vedantism and Christian Science have helped many, but have suffered the inevitable Nemesis of exaggeration. Vedantism in India, with its one Sole Reality, has coexisted with thirty-three million gods; with its denial of matter, suffering, and death, it has coexisted with the greatest material suffering and the highest death rate in the world at the present time. Christian Science has attempted to produce results of no pain, no sin, and no death. While this very attempt has brought release and healing to many, nevertheless it has brought into the movement a fringe of unreality. When the attempt is made to make life square with an impossible religious position, there is always the pressure to exaggerate the healings and minimize the failures, this, in spite of the evident sincerity of Christian Scientists. For it is an impossible position to wave all sickness, all suffering, all sin, all death out of existence as unrealities. If there is no such thing as suffering, then the cross of Christ is a travesty. We suspect any solution of the problem of suffering that leaves us with that result. No, the answer of Christian Science is a surface answer, and its steps are dogged by the inevitable Nemesis of superficiality. It is no chance that it has its greatest vogue among those person who are middle-age, comfortably well-off, where optimism is easy, and yet at the same time, where men and women are in need of assurance against the approaching dissolution of old age and death. But it is too superficial. In it there are no Wounds that will answer our wounds, no Death that will heal our deaths. A secular magazine had a cartoon on its front page, depicting two babies with boxing gloves on in the midst of a fray. The attention of one of one baby has been caught by two butterflies, flitting just above his head, and for the moment, he stands gazing at them, endangering himself to the blow, which his opponent is preparing to let fall on his unsuspecting nose. The little dog nearby, sees the impending tragedy, and with his tail between his legs, he winces as he waits for the inevitable blow to fall. Gazing at butterflies when the battle of life is on, is dangerous business. Any system that takes your attention off the grim facts of life, and creates a shallow optimism by calling attention to butterflies only, is doomed to be sent into an inevitable pessimism, as the blows of life fall. Christian Science and Vedantism create an initial optimism, as they gaze at the butterfly affirmations about life, but in the end, the blow falls and pessimisms result.

10. The Mistaken Attitude Among some Christians that Suffering is the Will of God and we are to Resign Ourselves to that Reality

This attitude of some Christians is scarcely to be distinguished from the attitude of Islam. The results are much the same, patience, resignation, and stagnation. This is not Jesus' view of human suffering as we will discover in the next chapter.

4

THE CHRISTIAN WAY: At Work in the Gospels

When we turn to the New Testament to find Jesus' way of meeting suffering, two things strike us with surprise: First, that his way is so utterly different from others. Second, that comparatively few in Christendom are really using it. We have let other streams of thought and outlook flow into the New Testament fountain, and we wonder why its taste is unsatisfactory, even bitter.

It reminds one of the Hindu youth who, when I asked him if he had a New Testament, gave the rather puzzling reply, "Yes, I have one somewhat." On this problem of meeting pain most of us have a New Testament somewhat! I feel sure that if we really got hold of its spirit and method, it would transform us. So, we turn to it with breathless interest, for there are few of us who do not need light and guidance at this place.

Jesus, after dealing with the matter of the man born blind, stood in the Treasury, which was the Court of the Women, and said, "I am the light of the world." At the place of money, gender, and of human suffering Jesus said he was the light of the world. These are really the outstanding problems of life, and to be "light" here is to be light indeed. Is it true?

Let us note that Jesus incidentally rejected, in the course of a positive statement about human suffering, three common attitudes about it. The disciples asked Jesus in the presence of the man born blind, "Who did sin, this man or his parents, that he should be born blind," and the Master answered, "Neither has this man sinned nor his parents. But that the works of God should be made manifest in him and I must work the works of him that sent me." Note that we have put a period after "parents," so that instead of reading, "Neither has this man sinned, nor his parents: but that the works of God should be made manifest in him," we read as above. This is allowable, some scholars say. If so, then we find that Jesus definitely rejects the idea that personal or parental sin is always at the back of all physical calamities, such as congenital blindness. The burden that weighs on many that their physical calamities are the punishment of God is thereby lifted. Sickness is not necessarily the sign of God's anger, or of his punishment. He also, according to this changed punctuation, refuses to accept the idea that God sends all suffering. The older punctuation implies that the disease is sent "that the works of God should be manifest in him." This would lay the responsibility for the sickness directly on God. Jesus rejects that. He refuses to throw the blame on the man born blind, or on his parents, or on God. He waves aside these assumptions and says that the calamity is an opportunity "to work the works of God" in him "while it is day." Jesus lays emphasis on the fact that calamity is opportunity. This gives us a key to his solution, a key to which we must return later.

Again, in the account where the people told him how Pilate had mingled the blood of the Galileans with their sacrifices, Jesus replied, "Think you that these Galileans were sinners above all the Galileans?

... I tell you, No. . . Or those eighteen, upon whom the tower of Siloam fell, were offenders above all the men that dwell in Jerusalem? I tell you, No." Here Jesus definitely says that the calamities that come from man (Pilate), and from the powers of nature (tower of Siloam falling), did not prove that the people who suffer from them were especially sinful. This takes away the self-righteous attitude of those who are free from calamities, when they view the calamities of others. It may be, said Jesus, that you are no whit better than those upon whom this trouble came.

Again, in connection with John being put into prison, the account says, "After that John was delivered up, Jesus came . . . preaching the gospel of God." Note: After the finest and truest of prophets had been put into prison and his witness silenced by an unjust king, Jesus came out preaching the good news about God! How can there be good news about a God who allows this sort of thing to happen? But that is exactly what Jesus did. He proclaimed good news, and he proclaimed it under those circumstances and about that God! This too gives us an inkling of his attitude.

In these three incidents Jesus definitely puts aside the idea that suffering is the result of the sin of a man in a previous birth (for how could his sin, except in a previous birth, cause him to be born blind?); and the idea that calamities which come from people like Pilate, and from the powers of nature, like the falling of the tower of Siloam, prove especial sinfulness, or, in fact, any sinfulness on the part of those who suffer them; and, lastly, Jesus rejects the idea that a man like John will be exempt from suffering, and that God isn't good when it happens otherwise. He proclaimed the good news in the very face of the happening. Evidently, his faith in the goodness and love of God was not built on foundations such as these. His faith must have been laid very deep, for it stood these shocks, and stood them triumphantly.

In the very center of the description in the twenty-first chapter of Luke, mentioned previously, concerning the nine roads from which suffering comes upon us, Jesus makes a declaration that throws a flood of light upon the whole problem and his attitude toward it: "It shall turn unto you for a testimony," or, as it has been translated, "It shall turn out for you as an opportunity for witnessing." In other words, Jesus says, you are to take hold of these calamities and turn them, i.e., use them for a testimony, you are not to escape trouble, nor merely to bear it as the will of God; you are to use it. Jesus suggests that we are to take up pain, calamity, injustice, and persecution, admit them into the purpose of our lives, and make them contribute to higher ends, the ends for which we really live. Jesus implies that the Christian has learned the secret of an alchemy by which the base metal of injustice and consequent suffering can be turned into the gold of character and into the gold of the purposes of the kingdom of God.

Jesus implies that the Christian has learned the secret of an alchemy by which the base metal of injustice and consequent suffering can be turned into the gold of character and into the gold of the purposes of the kingdom of God.

This presents to us a positive, active way of dealing with sorrow very different from the methods that really do not face up to life, but try to meet it by various subterfuges. There is an air of realism about the gospel, it refuses all shortcuts, all dodging of issues, all quackeries, all make believe, and faces life fairly and squarely and overcomes it. In nothing is this more truly illustrated than in the gospel's dealing with human suffering.

Jesus accepts the fact of human suffering. He does not explain it; much less does he explain it away. Had he undertaken to explain it; his gospel would have become a philosophy, in which case it would not have been a gospel. A philosophy undertakes to explain everything and then leaves everything as it was. Jesus undertook to explain little, but changed everything in sight. He did not bring a philosophy but a fact. The fact was his own method of meeting pain and injustice and transforming them into something higher. Out of this fact we gather up our philosophy. First fact, and then philosophy about the fact, that is the order. The Good News is not mere good views. It is the fact of sin and suffering being met and overcome and a way of life blazed out through them, this is the fact of the gospel.

When Jesus was hanging on the cross in dreadful suffering, someone tried to put a drug to his lips to deaden the pain. He refused it. He would take no dodging, no easy way out, no refusal to face the final issue, no opiates. He would match against the suffering and rejection of that hour, his inner courage of spirit, and turn the whole thing into a testimony. He would turn the world's supreme tragedy into the world's supreme testimony. And that he did.

When we turn to the Gospels, we find that almost everything beautiful there has come from something ugly. This principle of using things for a testimony is at work through the whole gospel from the beginning to the end.

Jesus goes into the wilderness "full of the Spirit," and undergoes a terrific strain of temptation for forty days. At the end of the forty days he emerges "in the power of the Spirit." Mere "fullness" had turned to "power" under the storm and stress of temptation. The whole intention of the temptations was to weaken him, to break him. In fact, they strengthened him, perfected him. He took these temptations up into the higher purposes of his life and made them contribute to his central aims. He turned temptation into a testimony. He used evil to fit himself to destroy evil!

The temptation of Job opens with his being delivered over to Satan to be tried, and after the stripping of Job it ends with him possessing twice as much as before. The temptation of Jesus opens with his conflict with the three subtle temptations, and ends with his emerging from them full of the power of the Spirit. The end was a character heightened in its spiritual perceptions and deepened in its capacity to share with others. Evil had turned to good. The temptation which had been intended to muddle his program had only clarified it.

> *The Good News is not mere good views. It is the fact of sin and suffering being met and overcome and a way of life blazed out through them, this is the fact of the gospel.*

Jesus went straight from the wilderness to the little synagogue at Nazareth to announce his program, "The Spirit of the Lord is upon me, because he anointed me to preach good tidings to the poor,..." Jesus could now announce that program because he himself was to be its illustration and embodiment. The temptation had made him more fit, and had made the program a more vital thing, for his own victorious spirit now throbs through the words. The words had become flesh.

That sense of victorious vitality, transforming everything into its own purposes, runs through the unfolding account. Did the Pharisees complain that he ate with publicans and sinners in close association, implying that he was of doubtful character than those with whom he ate? He turns that criticism into the matchless parables of the lost sheep, the lost coin, and the lost son. They flung this criticism upon him to break him, to discredit him in the eyes of the multitude, and he turns back this criticism into a revelation of the very heart of God. God's heart, he said, is like the shepherd's heart, which would seek for that one lost sheep until he finds it; like that woman and her search for the lost coin, Jesus would sweep the universe until he finds that one lost soul, lost in the dust of degradation; he stands upon the hilltops of Eternity, looking down the roads of Time, waiting, yearningly waiting for the return of prodigals to his forgiving heart.

It was a nasty fling for these religious leaders to make insinuations that would rob a man of the one precious thing of his life, his good name, and yet Jesus takes hold of that fling, and turns it for a testimony and a revelation of the very heart of Divine Reality. They would make him poorer by robbing him of his good name-- he makes us richer in our very conceptions of God by that very act. He did not bear the criticism, he used it.

A lawyer stood up to "tempt" him. He would also discredit him in the eyes of the multitude-- but the end? We have now the wonderful parable of the good Samaritan, and humanity has now ringing in its ears the challenging, searching words, "You must not pass by on the other side, when human need lies by the roadside." The inhumanity of the lawyer is turned and becomes a call and a command to show humanity to every man of every race. Jesus thus turns this malicious attempt into a testimony.

John the Baptist doubts Jesus and sends messengers to make further inquiries. To be doubted by your best friend, that is not easy. But Jesus takes that doubt and that questioning and makes religion a new, vital thing. He tells the messengers of John that they are to return and tell John what they had seen and heard. "The blind receive their sight, the lame walk, the lepers are cleansed, . . . and the poor have the gospel preached to them." The messengers of John had asked for the credentials of Jesus. "My credentials," said Jesus, "are not written in arguments; my arguments are these healed men." His credentials were written in the healed bodies and in the healed souls of men. His arguments were not in manuscripts but in man. This brings religion down from the academic discussion of validities to the facing of vitalities. That which is vital is valid. Jesus was giving life; therefore, he could claim to be life's Lord. When Elijah was standing on Mount Carmel, he said, "The God that answered by fire, let him be God." Jesus changed this test: "The God that answered by healed men, let him be God." What a cleansing breath this is to the musty atmosphere of religious discussion! But this clarification came out of a doubt, a doubt that hurt, the doubt of his friend, John.

One day a deeper doubt came and with it a deeper hurt. His very mother and kinsmen came to take him away, for they thought that be had lost his reason, that he was insane. One can stand almost anything from the outside if there is sympathy and understanding at home. But when the home misunderstands us, looks at us askance, greets us with coldness and suspicion, that is to be hurt indeed. The mother that bore him could bear with him no longer. So, they came to take him away. When Jesus heard that his mother and his brethren stood without desiring to speak to him, he waved his hand over the group about him and said, "Behold, my mother and my brethren! For whosoever shall do the will of God, the same is my brother, and sister, and mother." Here we find him announcing a deeper brotherhood, based not on blood, but on doing the will of God. It was the conception of the family of God, with God as the Father and men and women of every race and every clime who did the will of God as brothers and sisters. But note the situation in which he announces this concept: A man at the moment of being thought insane announces a world brotherhood, a world brotherhood that would cure the insanities of our narrowness of race and blood, our clashes of tribe and clan and nation, and would make our world a fit place for all persons to live in. A charge of insanity from his brothers becomes a charge to the world to live brotherly. Jesus turns the bitter suspicion of his family into a revelation of and a testimony to a larger family. Jesus did not bear this familial rejection, he used it.

Jesus turns the bitter suspicion of his family into a revelation of and a testimony to a larger family.

Jesus told those about him that he was going to "perform cures today and tomorrow" and "the third day" that he would be "perfected." He called his crucifixion being perfected! The worst that can happen to a man, crucifixion, turns out to him the best that can happen — perfection!

Jesus stood upon the Mount of Transfiguration and talked with Moses and Elijah about his death, which he was to accomplish at Jerusalem. As they stood there the topic of conversation was the cross – Jesus saw it in the dim distance, and he probably told Moses and Elijah that he would not ask to be excused, he would not step aside, but would go through with the whole thing. As they stood facing the cross, his whole being became luminous. He was transfigured before them. Here was something new: Life became luminous as it faced its direst tragedy!

The disciples would be arguing in the way, as to which of them should be greatest. They tried to shine by the assertion of claim and the magnification of themselves. But Jesus takes them to the mount and lets them see that life does not shine save as it faces its cross. They were trying to shine by self-assertion, and Jesus showed them that they would only shine by self-sacrifice. As they lost themselves, they would find themselves again. He was losing himself, but—-the luminous light! They fell on their faces before it.

As Jesus went before them toward Jerusalem, certain that he was to meet his death, his "disciples were amazed," amazed that a Man could go before them eager to meet that which human nature most shrinks from. Jesus stops only to heal, to teach, to inspire as he presses on his eager way. Peter tries to stop him, remonstrating that this shall never occur to him. But he tells Peter that he is a stumbling-block, and that he thinks as a man thinks and not as God thinks. Jesus thereby suggests that God thinks of and approves all this. What a God and what a representative Jesus is of him!

But in that moment a more bitter sorrow comes to Jesus. His disciples, whom he had prepared for this hour, and whom he had tried to infect with his spirit, now stop to quarrel over who should be first in the coming Kingdom. Quarreling over first places in the shadow of the cross of their Leader! This would surely break his spirit! But, no, Jesus turns even this for a testimony, for out of that quarrel comes to us the startling teaching that the greatest among us must be the servant of all. That one saying is enough to recast human society. And where did that teaching come from? A quarrel! Jesus used even the betrayal of his spirit to show forth a new spirit.

A deeper betrayal, the betrayal of Judas, only brings forth a deeper tenderness and a more glorious manifestation of a love that was not conditioned by the deed of the betrayal. "Love is not love which alters, when it, alteration finds." What Jesus had was love, for it did not alter when it found Judas altered from a disciple to a betrayer. But even that betrayal would only help toward the final end, and that final end would be victory. And it was victory! For Jesus did not bear the cross, he used it. There at the cross was the deepest injustice ever done, and Jesus turns it all into a healing of injustice and sin. These men were at their worst, and through it, Jesus reveals God at his best. There, at the cross, hate was bitterest, and there, at the cross, Love met it, and conquered it by taking it into his own heart and transforming it. The darkest hour of history becomes the lightest! The cross becomes a throne! The end, a new beginning!

5

THE CHRISTIAN WAY: At Work Among the Early Christians

Jesus seems at first sight to represent the passive tendencies toward life—withdrawal from the stings and hurts and entanglements of life. Did he not ask men not to be entangled with riches, to turn the other cheek when smitten, to go the second mile, to give the cloak also, to go forth as lambs in the midst of wolves, and to submit to the cross as he did? Jesus "seems" to meet life by withdrawal and submission. Yes, but only at first sight does he represent the passive attitude, for on second sight we find that Jesus represents the most amazingly active method of dealing with life.

Jesus withdraws from life only to advance further into life, he surrenders life only to get a better hold on it; he lets life do its worst, and then through it, shows the very best that God or man can demonstrate. Jesus takes on himself everything that speaks against the love of God, everything that makes the heart of man weep in desertion, every injustice that makes men cry out against the heavens, he takes all of this on himself at the cross, and through these very things shows the love of God.

But we are tempted to say "Yes, he did it; he met life when it was painfully cruel and transformed it, but that was his method; it cannot be ours." But that is exactly what his method did become. He transferred this vitality to his followers. The Acts of the Apostles represent the continuation of the acts of Jesus, especially in relation to the meeting of suffering and difficulty. To them, oppositions became opportunities, sufferings became songs.

The Acts of the Apostles is an hilarious book. It opens up with men so overflowing with spiritual vitality, that other men looking on, said that they were drunk. They were, but with the new wine of the Kingdom; a wine that left no "morning after" effect. The thing that made them bubble with new joy was the consciousness that they had sufficient inward resources to meet outer life.

Let us lift up out of the account a few of the incidents that illustrate this way of meeting suffering and opposition. Peter and John were going up to the Temple when a man sitting at the Beautiful Gate asked for alms. They probably fumbled in their pockets for something to give him, but found themselves in that "deepest of hells, the hell of an empty purse." Most of us would have let the incident stop right there, for what can you do if you haven't money in a world like this? We would have borne the pain of having nothing, a very acute pain to many. But these men did not stop there. Peter asked the man to look on them and then repeated the magnificent words, "Silver and gold have I none, but such as I have, I give thee. In the name of Jesus Christ of Nazareth, Rise up and walk." And the man did. These men did not bemoan their poverty, nor even bear it, they used it. They took up this poverty into the purpose of their lives and made it contribute to higher ends. The fact is that if they had had some money, they would have tossed him a coin, and that would have been the end of it, their adequacy on that level would have blocked a higher good. To many the loss of property and money during "the depression" has been unmitigated calamity, they have known life on no higher level, hence there is no way out. To others it has been an opportunity to transmute these losses into higher gain. They are more fit to run life's race because less corpulent. They have discovered that one's wealth may be in the abundance of one's possessions, or in the fewness of one's wants. They have learned to cultivate simple tastes and have found to their surprise that they have more life as they have less things. To many things lying lame within them, higher tastes, spiritual aptitudes, they have said, "Rise up and walk." And together with these they go into the temple of larger living.

If it seems remote to look at these disciples for examples, since they were chosen for a religious vocation, let us look at Stephen, a layman. As he sat before the Sanhedrin, they lied about him, twisted his words and attitudes, not an easy thing to bear. The fact is that Stephen did not bear this experience before the Sanhedrin, he used it! Every lie that fell upon him became light. "The people saw in his face the face of an angel." The more they lied about him the more Stephen shone. When they took him out and buried him beneath a shower of stones, in his dying prayer he prayed that this sin might not be laid to their charge. That prayer struck the conscience of a young man named Saul, bruised it, and finally led him to the feet of Christ on the Damascus road. They lied about Stephen, and he turned lies into light; they stoned him, and he turned the stoning into a testimony of unquenchable forgiveness, and in doing so, won to Christ the man who became the greatest Christian of the centuries. In misrepresentation and in death Stephen was stronger than his circumstances, and used them to further the Kingdom.

When persecution arose after the stoning of Stephen, the disciples were scattered by the fury of that persecution. But the result, "They that were scattered abroad went everywhere preaching the word." They were smitten by the hammer of unjust power, but the anvil upon which they lay was the anvil of God's purposes, and every blow that smote them, threw the sparks that scattered the fire. At the very same time they themselves were being smitten into shape to become keener instruments of the Divine Will. Inwardly, they became more fit and outwardly more effective. What can you do with a thing like that? You smite it and you scatter it.

Paul and Silas sat in an inner prison at midnight with feet and hands in stocks and their backs bleeding from cruel lashes. What had they done to deserve that punishment? Nothing, except that they loved humanity so much that they could not refrain from sharing with humanity the best they had. That best was Christ. But this was the result. So, did they sit there and complain that religion would not work, that God had let them down, that there was no justice in the universe, and that they were a sorry spectacle for their allegiance to it all. Did they do that? No, no, "At midnight Paul and Silas sang." Sang! Did song ever come out of the heart of deeper injustice and did it thereby ever have deeper meaning? They went higher and higher in their notes of praise, until they struck such high notes that God had to bring in the earthquake for a bass! Before morning the jailer was converted, the foundation of a Christian church was laid, and later on the man who was so deeply wronged in a Philippian jail wrote a letter to that church, a letter which today adorns our New Testament and enriches our spirits as we read it. They did not bear suffering, or try to escape it, they used it!

They did not bear suffering, or try to escape it, they used it!

The disciples were frustrated as they attempted to go into Asia, that frustration became the salvation of Europe. Balked at one place, they broke out in another. They turned their very frustrations into fruitfulness.

Taken before unjust tribunals to be tried, the disciples found there an opportunity to preach their gospel to royalty. Chained to soldiers, they spread through the Roman army the good news of a glorious freedom. Taken before Caesar to be tried, they led some of Caesar's household into the household of God.

Let us take one more incident out of the many of the New Testament, an incident that comes home to each of us at some time or another. Paul had a thorn in the flesh, a messenger of Satan to buffet him. From this description, it would seem that it was some physical infirmity that had come as a result of some wrong done to him, it was indeed a messenger of Satan to buffet him. It was an infirmity rooted in injustice, therefore, doubly hard to bear. Surely in a case of this kind God would heal the infirmity, cancel the injustice and let Paul get on with his work. Three times Paul requested God for its removal, and was refused. God seemed hard and indifferent. Injustice from man, plus infirmity in himself, plus indifference in God could equal a collapsed spirit. At least by all ordinary calculations it should. But it didn't for Paul! After the third request God said to Paul, "No, I will not heal you from this infirmity, but I will do something better. I will give you power to use it. My grace is sufficient for you, for my strength is made perfect in weakness." Paul, catching the significance of the offer, rose up and said, "Then, if that be the case, I will glory in my infirmities, for when I am weak, then am I strong." Blocked on the level of being healed, Paul saw the possibility of an opportunity on a higher level, namely, the level of using one's infirmities for the purposes of higher effectiveness.

That leads us straight face to face with the question of physical healing. It is obvious from the above account, that God does sometimes heal. Paul expected it. I think that we have a right to expect it. Some of us know enough of it in experience, so undoubtedly real that we cannot look on it as other than fact. We recognize that God heals in numerous ways, through nutrition, through medicines, through surgery, through mental suggestion, and through exercise. We cannot look on these as anything but divine methods. But over and above and beyond all that, there is the direct touch of the healing power of God upon the physical frame, that cannot be brought under the category of any of these. While this is true, we must also recognize that God does not always heal. It is in these exceptions that so many lose faith. It is in trying to prove that there are no exceptions, that a great deal of unreality and make-believe spring up and discredit the fact of divine healing. If we should recognize that sometimes God does heal and that sometimes he doesn't, and that the refusal to heal is in the interests of a higher good, then we can accept the refusal as being as much the gift of God as the healing. In fact, the refusal may mean a higher compliment than the healing, for in that instance God must refuse us on the basis that we can be trusted to use even infirmity. It is the compliment of his faith in our spiritual strength.

Those who are hurt at this point would have kept their faith and kept it more gloriously if they had seen the fact that God offers not one unalterable, fixed method of healing, but alternatives. The alternatives are these; either God will heal us from the infirmity or else he will give us power to use the infirmity. In either case it is a way out of the difficulty. When people ask me to pray that they may be healed, I always reply that I will, provided that in case God should refuse, they will not lose their faith in him. For I feel that it is more important that we keep our faith, than that we keep our health. With the faith intact even though healing is denied, we are ready for the alternative, namely, that we can employ the infirmity in the purposes of a higher good.

When a storm strikes an eagle, he sets his wings in such a way that the air currents send him above the storm by their very fury. The set of the wings does it. The Christian is not spared the pains and sorrows and sicknesses that come upon other people, but he is given an inner set of the spirit by which he rises above these calamities, by the very fury of the calamities themselves.

6

THE CHRISTIAN WAY: At Work Today

In the case of Jesus and the early Christians, there is something new and refreshing at work. First of all, there is displayed an absolute mental and spiritual honesty. There are no mental tricks to be played with suffering, however spiritual it may all seem to be. The gospel teaches honesty and forthrightness. There is little explaining and no explaining away. There is no concealing with its surface suggestions, there is no blinking of the stark facts, such as Christian Science proposes; there is no exaggerated statement of our being one with the Divine and therefore incapable of pain or suffering, such as Vedanta teaches; there is no paralyzing submission, such as Islam counsels; and there are no awful pessimisms, such as Buddhism leads us into, with its virtual denial of life itself, none of these are offered by the gospel. The New Testament offers a frank, open-eyed looking at life and letting life speak its direst word, and then taking hold of life at that point and turning the whole thing into victory.

There is at work here what one would call victorious vitality. Unless religion can manifest itself as victorious vitality it will be discarded, for everything from the lowest cell to the highest man is stretching up its arms after completion, after perfection, after more life. If religion stands as a denial of that process and a reversal of its aspiration, if it shows weariness and deserts the whole thing and asks men to get rid of the pains of life by various desertions and subterfuges, then it is doomed. It may linger on as an anesthetic to make easier the passing of a doomed people, but only as such. Its vitality will be gone.

But if this that Jesus offers is religion, then it stands amid that process of yearning after fuller life and expresses that yearning at its highest. Religion is a cry for life, for life in its highest qualitative terms. It is therefore far removed from any "escape mentality." Jesus was against anything that banked the native fires of life. We deny, therefore, that what he taught is what Schopenhauer called, "the denial of the will to live." It is, in fact, the will to live in its highest form. It expresses a yearning after a quality of life, as well as a quantity of life. It wants more life, and more life of a certain quality, not less. The answer to the problems of life is adequate life, not less life.

Someone asked a man in Manchester, England, why he drank liquor. He replied, "Because it is the shortest way out of Manchester." He had no courage to face Manchester, hence the shortest way out was by way of a bottle. In one swift hour Manchester, with its problems and pains was gone. He was free. But the difficulty with that remedy was that in the morning, when the effects of the liquor had worn off, Manchester was back again. And he had less vitality to face it, than the night before. All taking of drugs, all drinking of liquor, all taking to religious devotion and outlook that means a denial of life, are a failure of nerve.

The Communists of Russia say that "religion is the opiate of the people." When one looks at the type of religion they were facing in Russia in the Russian Orthodox Church, we are compelled to agree that there is some truth in what they say. It was an opiate, because it would not allow men to think, and because it stood back of the inhuman Czarist regime. Instead of standing with the people as they struggled for human rights, the religious leaders stood with prestige and privilege. But this type of religion they faced was far removed from the religion of Jesus and as contradictory to it as was the minister in India who, at a time of upset, administered communion to his European flock with a loaded revolver on the communion table, the loaded revolver said one thing and the Communion Table said another. The Russian Orthodox Church may have been an opiate to the people, but the religion of Jesus is not.

> *The religion of Jesus ... displays such an amazing vitality that there is no other word to use of it except victorious vitality.*

Dr. John Dewey, lecturing before a class of students, drew a line on a blackboard and on one side put all those systems of outlook and method that teach Control, and on the other side those that teach Acquiescence. On the Control side, he put Science, and on the Acquiescence side, he put Religion. To be fair he should have put "Some Religion." He might even have written "Some forms of Christianity." But certainly, he could not fairly have put the religion of Jesus. For it displays such an amazing vitality that there is no other word to use of it except victorious vitality. It gives one power to lay hold on the raw materials of life, good, bad, indifferent, just, unjust, pleasurable, painful, and to take them up into the life stream and assimilate them and use them. Plants and animals and men can survive as they assimilate things from their environment, which have an affinity with them.

They are dependent on affinities; if they are lacking, they die. But the Christian survives not only on affinities, but on oppositions, on infirmities, on pain, on crosses. He is, therefore, the hardiest of "hardy annuals;" rather, he is an evergreen. He therefore belongs to what James calls "the tough-minded" rather than to "the tender-minded." The Christian is the most pessimistic of men in that he views life through a cross, and the most optimistic in that he believes that behind every cross lies an Easter morning. In fact, he proceeds to turn his Calvary's into Easter mornings.

Lest we seem to be overstating the case before making it, let us look at this principle of victorious vitality at work, for it is not embalmed in the centuries, but is emblazoned in many a life now. It works wherever it is worked, and to the degree that it is worked. We shall take incidents from many cultures, from many differing types of Christian, from many ages, and from many differing sets of circumstances, to see if we can find from this widespread application, a possible universal principle at work.

I think I shall give the place of honor to a disabled woman in China. I stood one day speaking on this subject, and this woman occupied one of the front seats. Her disability was such that she could not see over the back of the bench. All the time I was speaking, there was a prayer in my heart that this woman would receive my message. But I found that I had wasted my sympathy, for she became a message to me! At the close a woman missionary came to me to introduce me to one of her teachers and she led me to this woman who had been in the front row for my talk. The woman must have seen the look of surprise in my face, for she said, "Yes, one of my teachers, and, moreover, one of the best I have ever had. In fact, she is the greatest spiritual power in this school, and has led more people to God than any other person in this city."

I was interested and urged her to go on. She told me how as a child she had been dropped by careless hands and her back broken, and how for many years after that she was a bad-tempered young woman lashing with the sharpness of her tongue against her fate and her environment. And no wonder, for she seemed to have a good case for bad temper, and revolt against a universe that would let a thing like that happen, when she had done nothing to merit it. But one day, she let Christ into her embittered soul and lo, all was changed. To the astonishment of everyone, she decided to be a teacher. When Christ comes into the heart, it is amazing to see how life takes on a seriousness of purpose. It begins to push the clods from off its head, as it responds to the urge toward the light, toward blossoms and fruitfulness. This woman felt that urge and became a teacher, but when she was sent to a village to take charge of a school, there was almost a riot by the villagers, who supposed her disability to be an ill omen. But the missionary insisted that they try her, promising that if they did not like her as a teacher, she would take her back. The villagers reluctantly agreed. When after several years the missionary came to take her away to a larger school, there was almost a riot again; these villagers insisted that they had never had such a teacher, for she radiated the love and power of God. She had taken her disabled body and had made it the instrument of a regnant spirit. The last I saw of her was as she pushed the little bamboo stool in front of her, as she worked her way across the room. That stool served as her crutches, and it was upon that stool that she sat to teach, and it is upon that stool that she sits, as Christ each day crowns her with a crown of life.

It is her throne. The symbol of her infirmity becomes the place of her crowning.

Let us turn from this account of one to whom personally a wrong had been done, to an incident where a wrong is done to those whom we love, —- sometimes harder to bear than the first. It is comparatively easy to forgive an injury to ourselves, but when it is done to those whom we truly love, the sting goes deeper and it is hard to eradicate. A missionary family, consisting of father and mother and three children, were all murdered in what was known as the Vegetarian Riots in China. Four of the other children escaped, after seeing the rest of the family murdered. They met again and decided what their revenge would be; they would all go and get the best training possible and then return to China, and give their lives in service for those who had murdered the rest of the family. They did so. All of them returned to China and have spent years of fruitful, loving service to the land that had been so unjust to the rest of the family. One of these brothers won to Christ Dr. James Yen, affectionately called "Jimmy Yen," the father of the Mass Education Movement in China, a movement through which literally hundreds of thousands are being taught to read. Alongside of the five graves in Foochow, are two others, graves of the daughters of a widowed mother in Australia. They too had been murdered at the same time. When the news came to the widowed mother that her daughters had been murdered, her response was that, as she had no other daughters to give, she herself would go. So, at sixty-two years of age she sold off all that she had, went to the place where her children had been murdered, learned the language, set up a school, gave twenty years of service, and dying at the age of eighty-two, was buried beside her daughters. These five survivors concerned in this deep injustice and cruel wrong did not bear their pain, they harnessed it and made it serve. Instead of being dragged to the chariot wheel of fell circumstance, they mounted the chariot, seized the reins and drove it to their own destination. And a glorious destination it was!

Sometimes unjust suffering hits us personally, sometimes those whom we love, and sometimes our work. A doctor in China had built up an efficient hospital through years of toil and self-sacrifice. When the Communist wing of the Nationalist army swept northward, they looted his hospital and left it the shell of what it had been. All the work of years went down in a crash. Not an easy thing to forgive! But, undaunted, he followed the army and attended to its sick and wounded. When General Chang Kai Shek, who was in charge of the army, saw this, he asked his wife, "What makes this foreign doctor tend to the sick and wounded, when these very men destroyed his hospital?" His wife, who was a Christian, replied, "It is Christianity." Said General Chang, very thoughtfully, "Then, I must be a Christian." This was one of the three influences that made the General, then President of China, decide to become a Christian at a time when the Anti-Christian Movement was sweeping China. This undoubtedly, as his wife assured me, turned the tide against the Anti-Christian Movement and helped to bring about the present [1933] very favorable attitude of China toward Christianity. The Anti-

> *A doctor's work was destroyed by selfish and brutal soldiers, but instead of complaining at the lack of interest that God has in his children... he turned it for a testimony.*

Christian Movement has spent itself. China has decided not to be anti-Christian, but she has not yet decided to be Christian. She is in the moment of the Great Hesitation. The situation is in the hands of the Christian Church to do with it what it will.[1]

A doctor's work was destroyed by selfish and brutal soldiers, but instead of complaining at the lack of interest that God has in his children and their work for him, instead of merely bowing and bearing it, the doctor turned it for a testimony, and through this calamity helped to open the greatest evangelistic opportunity in the world at the present time. That looted hospital has been reconditioned and the doctor is doing splendid service, but he undoubtedly did more by the way he met this calamity than he could have done if life had not called on him to go through the pain of seeing everything go down in a crash. The revelation of a spirit in a moment of time probably did as much, or more, to set up a light before men than a whole lifetime of untroubled service.

General Feng Yu Shiang has been in eclipse as a Christian for some time. He had been hit hard, so he told me, by the events of the last few years, especially by the imperialistic attitude of some outside nations. He has nearly gone under. But one thing, he told me, has held him strong. One of Feng's relatives killed Doctor Logan, a missionary doctor, who was attending this relative as his patient. It seemed an unrelieved tragedy. But Mrs. Logan, a trained nurse, took charge of the patient who had killed her husband and nursed him back to health. Logan's son was in America studying, and when Feng heard that he was working his way through college, he gathered together two thousand dollars and sent the money to the son to help him with

1 The situation has now changed quite dramatically and what appeared favorable to Christianiy in China during Jones' writing of this book is no longer the same. Editor.

his educational expenses. The family, however, felt that they could not keep it, so they returned it, thanking the General very heartily, but saying that they felt the son must work his way through college with his own hands. "Now," said Feng, as we stood on the side of the sacred mountain of Taishan and looked out across the valley, "that is real Christianity. That has hold of me very deeply." General Feng held my hand a long time as we stood there, and as I looked into his rugged, honest face, I felt that he would one day come back again to a living Christian faith, and that if he did, he would be stronger than ever, for he has in him the raw materials of being a really great Christian. If he does come back, the spirit of that wife and son, who turned their experience into a testimony, what seemed like an unalloyed tragedy, will lead the way. But if he doesn't come back, if the whole thing seems unrelieved failure, nevertheless the spirit itself which they have shown is the victory. Whether another rises from the dead through it or not, that spirit is deathless, it cannot fail. Whether General Feng is lifted by it or not, the rest of us are.

Here are the two greatest military men of China, Generals Chang and Feng, conquered by the turned cheek. What military force could not do; an invincible love did. The Christian is called on to use subtle forces that make military power seem impotent and absurd. As someone has said, "To strike back when struck arouses the combative instinct in your antagonist, to run away when struck, arouses the hunting instinct in the pursuer, but to turn the other cheek arouses the deeply tender instincts in him." Along this line lies victory.

Simon, the Cyrenian, came out of the country one day little dreaming of the tragedy into which he would be thrust by circumstances. But he found himself being taken hold of by violent hands, and a cross thrust upon his shoulders. "Him they compelled to bear the cross." The tragedy had a sharp point in it for Simon, in view of the fact that the Roman soldiers would not lay hands on one of their own countrymen, for that would have been a degradation to him; nor would they lay hold of a Jew, for that would have been a possible point of offense to an already embittered nation, so they laid hold on an African, the "weakest" member of society, who had no way of retaliation, and made him bear the cross that other shoulders would have refused. A personal humiliation, combined with a racial wrong, must have cut deep into the soul of Simon. But as he trudged up the hill that day, he learned life's deepest lesson, for he saw Jesus turning the whole bitter shame into a triumph of love. As in a flash, he too caught the way to deal with this tragedy, and turned the whole thing into something else that transformed it and him, so much so that he passed it on to his sons, Alexander and Rufus. These sons became sufficiently prominent in the early church to be mentioned in the Gospels in such a way, that it was taken for granted that they were well known. The tragedy was transformed, and so were Simon and his sons.

Life often deals with us as it dealt with Simon; we walk out into a cloudless day, the birds are singing as we went our way "from the country," all life seems full of hope and promise. Then suddenly, we find ourselves in the midst of tragedy; circumstances lay on us a heavy cross, and we are compelled to trudge up some lone Calvary bearing a cross of unchosen pain. But if life deals with us as it did with Simon, we can deal with life as Simon did. That cross threw him in company with Jesus, and that brief moment with Jesus gave him power to transform a racial wrong into the righting of a race, beginning with himself and his sons. His racial heredity was responsible for his bearing an unwanted cross, but he uses it to begin a new heredity. He becomes the first of the great African race to begin the long march up from slavery to freedom. The cross that he bore became the banner that goes before them, the symbol alike of their shame and their glory.

In their upward march they have set their sorrows to songs, and out of the heart of pain, have sung "the Negro spirituals," the most triumphant music the world has ever produced. "Nobody knows the trouble I see, Glory, Hallelujah!" The people who can begin their song the way that song begins and end it the way it ends are headed for glory, both here and hereafter. When the Burma Gospel Team of students came to India singing "Negro spirituals," I said to myself, "These high-brow Indians will not take this sort of spiritual singing." They took it! It swept India by storm. Everyone can understand and appreciate a triumphant spirit, no matter in what words it clothes its song.

Everyone can understand and appreciate a triumphant spirit, no matter in what words it clothes its song.

A friend of mine, riding horseback through a sparsely populated portion of Virginia, came suddenly into a clearing in which stood a cabin with an African-American woman in the doorway. The friend called out greeting, asking who lived there. The reply came happily back, "Nobody but me and Jesus." That woman standing in the doorway of her lonely cabin, bereft of all her loved ones, but with a light on her face never seen on land or sea, and with the words, "Me and Jesus," upon her lips, is a queen, no matter what her circumstances may say. She belongs to that succession of Simon, who toil up the hill with crosses of racial and personal wrong laid on their shoulders, but singing, "Nobody knows the trouble I see," and ending with an Easter morning note of "Glory, Hallelujah!"

In Peking there is a beautiful temple, solidly and massively built over the tomb of a prime minister of one of the Manchu emperors.

They say that this tomb and this temple were built over the body of the prime minister to keep down his spirit, to prevent its rising to the throne. Many an institution, such as slavery, has been built over the spirit of man to keep it from rising to the throne of human dignity and freedom. But the former slaves are everywhere singing their way out of tombs to thrones of freedom. When I first heard Hawaiian music, there was such a plaintiveness in it that I turned to a friend and said, "That is tears set to music." I did not know then that this music was invented by the lepers of Hawaii. When I learned that, then I knew why it was that it touches us so deeply. It is deep answering deep.

Leper asylums are usually depressing places, but I once came away from one with my heart singing. There was a person with leprosy there who had been a Christian worker, but was stricken in the prime of life with the dread disease. His fingers had all been eradicated by the disease except the stump of his right-hand index finger. That was all that was left. But in the stump of that finger, he grasped the bow of a violin and played most exquisitely and triumphantly. I inwardly saluted him. He commanded my spirit. Did I say he "was" a Christian worker, nay, he "is" a Christian worker, and the spirit that can use the stump of a leprous finger to grasp the bow of a violin, is doing more Christian service than many an unscarred ministry. That leper was "framing out of three sounds, not a fourth sound, but a star." And that star was guiding us.

In the city of Rangoon was a bright, vivacious European college girl who became a teacher. Life seemed to hold beautiful promise for her, but before her sun had climbed to its zenith it became suddenly darkened by the blackest of clouds. She discovered that she had contracted leprosy. She tried to hide the dread fact, but it could not be done. She was taken away for treatment. After some time, she came back symptom-free. She began her teaching again. But the disease had only been stayed; it was still there and began to be active again. She felt instinctively that if she went back for treatment again, it would all be over. She tried to smother it and tell herself that it was not there, but to no avail. One day she deliberately left her classroom, walked out the two miles to the leper asylum, hesitated a long time before the gates, knowing that if they closed on her this time, it would be almost certainly for good and all. With a prayer on her lips she went in. On the axis of that prayer, life turned from resentment and bitterness to victory. Blocked from teaching on the outside, she turned to teaching the lepers and more, she arranged them into a choir and taught them to sing. And in doing so, her own heart caught a strange new music it had never known before. She is radiant. Did I say she was teaching those lepers? Nay, she is teaching us all. Every picture must have its dark background to set off the foreground, so she used the shadows of this affliction as the background upon which she paints a luminous spirit. When we learn to teach others at this place, we are really teaching, for we are not imparting information but transformation.

These are dramatic phases of the Victory. But they are not, thereby, more real than some of the silent ones, unheralded and unseen. The unseen crosses that press in upon the spirit are often more poignant, than those that cut into the flesh. Of all those who suffer in silence, the most silent must be those who go through life without finding a mate. The human spirit is made for companionship and feels lost and unhappy until it finds its counterpart. But what of those who never find?

I remember one such, who seemed to be the very epitome of gracious womanhood. She had every instinct for motherhood, and what a mother she would have been! But she, who would have made such a wonderful mate, was denied a mate, and she who would have been a model mother, was denied motherhood. The sight of a babe upon another woman's breast sent a pain through her soul, like the piercing of Mary's sword. She bore this unseen cross in silence during the years. They were not lonely years, for they were filled with beautiful service to others. But there was always the gnawing. One day as she listened to an address describing the birth of a human spirit from darkness and shadows to new light and life, she saw a vision and heard a call. She would give herself to the bringing forth of spiritual children, nursing them into character and fruitfulness. She, who was denied motherhood on one level, could give herself to motherhood on another. No pain and travail would be too terrible to bring forth these spiritual children into the world. The gnawing, regretful pain has gone and a creative pain, a pain that is really joy set to a higher key, has taken its place. Regret has turned to recreation. She is a happy mother, mothering the souls of the lowly and finding a mate in human need, married to misery, yet blissfully happy. She is using her denials and turning them into doors.

Psychology is teaching us the possibility of the sublimation of instincts, rather than their suppression. They tell us that the sexual instinct can be turned into creative forms of art and poetry and service. This is all to the good, and as such we welcome it. But psychology, dealing with less than the highest, is not able to put the sublime into its sublimations. It teaches sublimation, but must wait on religion to put content into it. Jesus takes all balked instincts and sets them to glorious tasks in the new Kingdom. There these instincts are free, because free now to express themselves in their highest forms. Pugnacity becomes persistence in standing for the right, fear becomes reverence for God and human personality, sexuality becomes creative tenderness in service, self-love becomes a larger love of selves, gregariousness becomes human brotherhood.

Nothing is thrown away. It is all turned to higher forms. "Christianity is the only religion that throws nothing away," including frustration and pain and suffering. Jesus said to his disciples, "Gather up the fragments that remain, that nothing be lost." He redeems not only human souls, but also the fragments that remain when life goes to pieces under the blows of suffering and sorrow and frustration.

In the parable of the wedding feast of the king's son, those who were invited refused on one pretext or another. Then the king sent out and called in the halt and the lame and the blind and filled his feast. Christianity uses its very oppositions to fulfill its own program. The specially privileged were first invited, but when they refused, the servants were sent out to get "as many as you can find." By the refusal of the specially privileged, the invitation broke out into democratic universality and thus fulfilled its essential nature, fulfilled it by a frustration!

The gospel is a gospel of "in spite of." People take it not because it is an easy, but a victorious, way to live. If someone is looking to the gospel to be a way "on account of," he or she will probably be puzzled and disappointed; but if she is looking to it as a way "in spite of," then she will find that she has laid hold on adequate vitality.

7

THE CHRISTIAN WAY IS VICTORY

We have seen that Jesus presents to us the possibility of an active dealing with sorrow, in deep contrast to the usual passive method. The verse usually quoted by the proponents of the passive method is the prayer of Jesus in Gethsemane, "Not my will, but thine be done." That, they say, is the high-water mark of religion in general and of prayer in particular. The usual connotation of "Thy will be done" is "Thy will be borne," a passive acquiescence. Heiler quotes the prayer of a Native American who lost his three tobacco pipes, a greater loss is inconceivable to an Indian, and in his distress turned to the Great Spirit, saying, "O great God, thou who seest everything, and upholdest everything, grant, I pray thee, that I may find what I seek." Then, after expressing his desire, he leaves the fulfillment of the prayer to the Great Spirit, ending in these words, "and yet let thy will be done." Heiler, commenting, says: "Here the petition ends in submission. The highest and finest prayer which the history of religion knows, comes from the lips of a pious Native American."

I once went into the Garden of Gethsemane, there to spend the night in prayer, centering my whole meditation on what I thought was the heart and substance of the Gethsemane event, "Not my will, but thine be done." I expected to come away chastened, submissive, surrendered. But in those silent hours, I found my thought shifting to the words of Jesus to the sleepy disciples, "Arise, let us be going," let us be going to meet the betrayal, the rejection, the accusations, the spittle, the cross. The will of God was to be done, not by acquiescence, but by activity, it was to be done by taking hold of the whole miserable business and turning it into a triumph of the love of God. That was what it meant by the will of God being done, that will was active, redemptive, breaking through in love to men, in spite of their cruelty and hate. "Arise, let us be going," to meet the whole thing is the key to the words, "Thy will be done." I came away from Gethsemane, not depressed into submission, as I thought I would be, but with a battle-cry sounding in my heart. Gethsemane meant to me no longer a sigh and a tear and a submission, but the call to arise and be going to meet everything, even the very worst that can happen to us, and to turn it into a testimony of the love of God. We can see Jesus in Gethsemane no longer as the Victim of the will of God, but the Victor through that will.

The will of God was to be done, not by acquiescence, but by activity, it was to be done by taking hold of the whole miserable business and turning it into a triumph of the love of God.

From that moment on Jesus assumed command of every situation. He healed the ear of the man who came to arrest him. He pronounced the doom of every kingdom, founded on blood and fear, in the words, "They that take the sword shall perish with the sword." By the terror of his silence he made Pilate tremble on his throne, — the Accused judged the judge, and with him his whole empire. Jesus would not accept the tears of the weeping multitude, he told them to weep for themselves and for their children. He dispensed paradise to a dying thief on a nearby cross, and commended his murderers to the mercy and forgiveness of God. At the end he cried, "It is finished," the will of God had been done, — done in spite of the hate of men, yes, through it, and that will was redemptive love.

We repeat, then, that this is victorious vitality. It is the art of living dangerously. A Hindu student, after reading Nietzsche's book on living dangerously, came to his orthodox father and said: "I have been impressed with the necessity of living dangerously. I want to practice it. Please get me a motor cycle." To him to live dangerously was to dodge traffic on a motor cycle, but this is to live dangerously in a very harum-scarum, surface sort of way. Western life is tinged with that kind of attempt to live dangerously. Jesus would call us to sound the depths of life and to live dangerously there, to grapple with the great issues of life and to show life through them.

Heiler is right when he says that "prophetic religion is an irresistible will to live, an uncontrollable impulse toward expression, mastery, and exaltation of the sense of living." The faith of Jesus is like the plant that lays hold of the muck and filth of things, and transforms them into exquisite color and form in the beauty of the flower. It has within its depths a quenchless "Hope, till hope creates, from its own wreck, the thing it contemplates."

Some types of Christianity have often tried to sustain character and joy out of the contemplation of the rewards of heaven. Now, there is no doubt that the Gospels do teach compensations, beyond this life, in heaven. But its emphasis does not lie there. It produces its character and its joy out of and amid conditions here and now. Therefore, the type of character it produces when fully in operation, has rosy cheeks and tingling blood from the facing of biting winds. A character produced out of heaven, contemplating compensations, is anemic and pale, lacking robust life, very like the flower in the cellar living in anemic contemplation of the sunshine above. No, Christianity bids us make heaven out of our hells.

Prayer should take us out of our dark corners, and help us to turn our infirmities into ladders that reach to heaven here and now.

I once saw a man spreading his prayer mat in a dark corner under a stairway and prostrating himself in prayer there with his face to the floor. The stairway led to the sunlight and the open vista above. But his face was to the ground, contemplating the joys that Allah would grant him in heaven. I wanted to take him by the hand, to lead him out of the dark corner up the open stairway to the sunlight above, and let him face life with God there. Prayer should take us out of our dark corners, and help us to turn our infirmities into ladders that reach to heaven here and now. The faith of Jesus is the highest expression of the will to live. But it is not a will to live with a set jaw and a drawn countenance and a strained attitude toward life. It is a restful will to live, for its will is possessed by Life, and there is a quiet confidence within, that shows no fear of life or anything that it can do.

A student said he always went to chapel service at the university when a certain man was to speak, "for," said he, "he stands up there with a quiet confidence and deals with the great issues of life like a Christian who holds four aces in his hand." The student was expressing in very modern terms the fact of confidence, that the Christian has sufficient resources to meet life no matter how hard the game of life is played against him.

To those who think that Jesus taught the denial of the will to live we answer that the phrase "he that loseth his life shall find it," contradicts this idea, for here Jesus asserted that the "self" or "life" is found. The renunciation of the self leads to the realization of the self. We let go the smaller self to gain a larger self. It "results in the absolutizing of the self. It is a sublimation of the will to live." As Paulsen says, "Every self-sacrifice is at the same time self-preservation, namely, preservation of the ideal self." We are suppressed on one level of life, in order to express ourselves on a higher level. We accept a law to gain a liberty, a liberty through that very law.

The Christian has sufficient resources to meet life no matter how hard the game of life is played against him.

This was beautifully expressed in a Christmas letter written to me by a disabled person. "How can I be free? Law there is, and I must reckon with it and its penalties. Am I not bound to obey law? As I ponder the question, Tagore's story of the string comes to mind and gives me light. A violin string lies on the table. It is under no constraint. We might think it free. But is this mute thing free? Put the string in its place in the violin. It is bound. When set in motion, it gives out dull sounds. But draw it tighter. Stretch it up to key. Let it be swept by Kreisler's bow. Now it is free. It sings."

"Jesus stretched his life upon the cross and swept it with his love, God, the Song!"

The man who wrote those lines was himself being stretched daily on a cross of pain, but his being too was swept by the love of God, and some of us who heard the music pause gratefully and say, "God, the Song!"

A writer who had suffered a great deal, was heard by a friend to pray for release from the suffering. The friend put his hand lovingly on his shoulder and said, "If that prayer is answered, it will spoil your English style." The friend knew that no man could write as he did except out of the heart of pain. Someone who heard a great vocalist sing remarked, "What a wonderful voice she would have, if something would break her heart!" She needed what we all need, namely, a Hand that will draw our heart-strings tighter to get the best music out of us.

One of the finest types of missionaries lived and labored in the South of India, and amid the multitude of things, which fell to his lot to do, was to tear down a leper's house. While on furlough he developed leprosy. At first, he was stunned, his faith tottered and came near falling. Why had God allowed this to come upon him? To him who was in the prime of life and dedicated to a missionary task that needed him? But his faith righted itself, and he saw through the gloom. He got hold of what is the spiritual counterpart of the invention called an "All-weather sextant," an invention by which the sun can be seen by the mariner no matter what clouds or mists may hide it. He took this spiritual "All-weather sextant" and saw God's face through the clouds. Isolated from man, God seemed nearer. Friends visited him in his isolation to learn from him the way to live. For he had found the way to live, "in spite of." But one friend came from India with pity in his heart, and showed by the tone of his voice that he was pitying him. The man with leprosy stopped him: "You are feeling sorry for me, and you must not do it. I have never known deeper joy in my life. These walls are radiant with the love of God." God did not heal him of his leprosy, but God did something better: he healed others through him, healed them at the place where we most need healing, in our spirits.

In one of our Round Table Conferences, a very fine Christian gave the following as his view of what religion meant to him in experience: "I have found that if you follow Christ, three things will happen to you: First, you will be delivered from all fears. Second, you will be absurdly happy. Third, you will have trouble." It seemed an anticlimax to say that the final thing is that you will have trouble, but I am persuaded that he is right. You cannot be delivered from all fears, nor can you be absurdly happy, unless you have learned to accept trouble and use it. It is of no use to tell people not to be afraid, for they know there is something to be afraid of. Even if they know that there is nothing to be afraid of, they have inner fears that cannot be controlled by good counsel. A Hindu student said to a friend of mine, "My mind tells me that there is nothing in that idol to be afraid of, but my heart is very afraid." There were unreasoning fears that were deep down. The only way to get rid of those fears is to be convinced that if the worst happens, it can be turned into the best. The leper had been delivered from all his fears, because the worst had happened, but life, the real life within, was intact. It is "absurd" to be as happy as a person felled by leprosy, but the gospel teaches that glorious absurdity.

Among a group of students who came from Burma to India as a Gospel team, or Group Fellowship, was one whom they called "The Buffalo." He was as strong as a buffalo, hence the name. Along with this strength he had a very quick temper, a dangerous combination. The last thing he did before he was converted was to break with one blow, three ribs of a man who angered him. This Group had finished their five months' tour of the colleges in India, and as I sat with them, I asked them what was the outstanding, the happiest moment of the tour. We went around the circle and each told of the happiest moment, and when it came to the turn of "The Buffalo" he said in a simple, straightforward way: "One night a student followed us out of the meeting and as I sat in the motor car, he came deliberately up to me and spat in my face. Now, before this tremendous thing called conversion happened to me, I would not have hesitated a second in knocking him down. But the strange thing is that I did not even feel like doing it, and, moreover, I look back on that as the happiest moment of the whole tour." It was said without triteness or boasting. He was reporting a fact. Now, it is "absurd" to be happy when one spits in your face, and yet that is exactly what the gospel offers.

Jesus strikes the deepest note in life. Our modern churches do not strike that note.

One of the Church Fathers could say to his opponents concerning the sufferings of the early Christians: "Every man who witnesses this great endurance is struck with some misgiving. He is set on fire to look into it to find the cause of it. When he has learned the truth, at once, he follows it himself." "Follows it himself," it is "absurd" to follow a thing that causes suffering, and yet we know instinctively that Jesus strikes the deepest note in life. Our modern churches do not strike that note. They appeal to comfort and wonder why the churches are empty. They have swept out of the Protestant churches the crucifixes, and have put in cushions. Then they wonder why the cushions are not used. Jesus appeals to the heroic, and millions would die for him today.

A proud Manchu woman resisted all Christian appeals although her husband had become Christian. Persecution broke out against the Christians and she had to flee along with her husband to the mountains. There they suffered untold hardships. In the midst of it, she decided to become a Christian. "Any religion that is persecuted this way must be true," was the way she put it. She became a wonderful follower of Christ, driven to his side by the wounds she found there.

It is "absurd" for people to sing, when they are falling to their death, but that is exactly what the Christians did when the great persecution broke out against them in Madagascar. They were hung over a cliff by a rope and told, that if they did not recant, the rope would be cut. They refused to recant and the rope was cut, and again and again they were heard singing, as they fell through the air to their death.

Dean Inge says that "Joy as a moral quality is a Christian invention." This is true because into the Christian joy was put a moral quality that made it different. It was joy which represented a moral conquest. The moral conquest gave it a moral quality.

This kind of joy is different from amusement. The latter is from the outside in, while the former is from the inside out. Happy people do not need to be amused. They have springs within them. In a moment of disillusionment, I wrote these lines:

"At the heart of every earthly thing,
There is a sting, there is a sting."

But now I have learned to write in answer:

"When every earthly thing
Leaves its bitter sting,
My heart has learned to sing!"

When one can write the first, he is Buddhist in his attitude; when he can write the second, he is learning to be Christian.

Much of the modern attempt to find joy through amusement reminds us of the old lady who took some children to a circus, and when one child, through the strangeness of the various happenings, began to cry, she grabbed the child by the back of the neck and shook him, saying, "I brought you here to enjoy yourself, now enjoy yourself,—-do you understand?" And she shook him again, to give emphasis to her demand that the child enjoy himself. Many moderns are shaking their poor, starved, weeping souls and trying thereby to make them enjoy themselves! When a man has to say to his soul, "Eat, drink, and be merry," as the rich man did, then we know that he is not merry. Modern hedonism has brought a sad, disillusioned world into being.

Joy is written in the constitution of things, in the very constitution of our faces. They tell us that it takes sixty-four muscles of the face to frown, but only fourteen to smile, —then why overwork your face! God has thrown the emphasis on the side of joy, by making the human face take the line of least resistance when it takes the side of joy. But the face that has joy in the New Testament sense, has no cheap joy. There is in it no make-believe or "made-joy." Justice Chandavakar, a very noble Hindu, once said of Keshab Chunder Sen, a leader of the Brahmo Samaj, that he had "a New Testament face." One Hindu says of another Hindu that he has "a New Testament face." Whatever it was that made up the New Testament face, certainly it was obvious that it could not be identified with professionalism. Keshab, though not a Christian by profession, had looked at Christ until he had caught something of his joy. Just what is "a New Testament face"? It is a face where the lines have turned to light, where grief has learned to smile through its tears, and where in spite of everything, there is the sense of victory.

Jesus said, "These things have I spoken unto you, that my joy may be in you, and that your joy may be fulfilled." Here we find two joys meeting each other. The one is "my joy," a joy from the outside; the other, "your joy," a joy from the inside. I say this joy of Jesus is from the outside, and yet it is so inward and intimate that it too, can be said to be from within. The divine joy meets the human joy: the one from above fills, and the other from below is fulfilled. They are made for each other, and the human soul in finding this joy finds its very life. Ordinarily, the mystic would say that the divine joy is everything and the human joy is nothing. The Barthians for once, would agree with the mystics. But in Jesus' statement both are preserved. The human is not swamped in God, but is fulfilled in him. Since both are preserved, it shows that we are made for his joy, and when we find it, we find our own fulfilled. The New Testament face is a face that is supernaturally natural.

Barry tells us that "there is always throughout Greek literature a haunting sense of melancholy, a sense of frustration and unfulfillment." They protested that they believed in the joy of life, but it was never fulfilled, for they could never see any ultimate reason for joy. No man can be ultimately joyful unless he feels that his joy is an ultimate joy. "The Greeks expressed a glorious confidence in man, but gave no ground for believing in man." They had not seen a man as "a man for whom Christ died."

Some doctors were about to operate on a poor patient and one of them thoughtlessly remarked, "Bring on the worthless creature," thinking the patient to be unconscious. But the patient, a learned man, though now in straitened circumstances, replied, "Do you call him 'worthless,' a man for whom Christ died?" The worth of a man is now deepened by the worth of the One who died for him. We therefore believe in man because we believe in the Man, and so, our joy has meaning, since touched by his joy. The Greeks knew nothing of the kind of joy of One who standing in the shadow of his cross could say, "My joy." Our joy is founded on that joy which has stood the shocks, and still sings. No man can sing unless he feels that his song is sounding the depths of the universe. The Christian founding his joy on a cross, and finding it through a cross, is sure that in that cross he is striking the deepest note that life can strike. It is the bass note of his song; and if, having struck that lowest note, he then goes on to strike the highest notes of joy, we know that without that lowest note the highest could not be struck. But together, they bring out the harmony of the whole.

The Christian founding his joy on a cross, and finding it through a cross, is sure that in that cross he is striking the deepest note that life can strike.

The Chinese have an inscription over the glorious Jade Fountain in Peking, "Under Heaven, the First Spring." As earthly springs go, I suppose it is the most wonderful that the world possesses. But as I gazed into its crystal depths, I said to my friend, "This is glorious, but the Christian has discovered the real, 'Under Heaven, the First Spring,' for he that drinks of these waters shall thirst again, but he that drinks of the waters that Christ shall give to him shall never thirst; but the waters that Christ shall give to him shall become in him a well of water, springing up unto everlasting life." That is "the First Spring," for it has its source in a hill called Calvary. It is joy out of suffering. At Shanhaikwan, where the Great Wall meets the sea, there is an inscription over the gate, "Under Heaven, the First Gate." The Manchu emperors who put the inscription over the Spring and the inscription over the Gate are gone, the palace of the Jade Fountain is in the hands of others, and the First Gate is in the hands of the Japanese, thus do earthly "firsts" all let us down, but this joy that Jesus gives has the feel of the eternal in it, it springs up unto everlasting life.

The Christian has, therefore, what Von Hugel called "an overflowing interior plenitude." He knows what J. A. Symonds is talking about when he says that his concentration and unification enable him "to hire sunshine for leaden hours," and "to engender a mood of mind, sufficient for the purposes of living." The Christian knows this, and more, for what he has found is not a "mood of mind," but inward resources of the spirit, an overflowing interior plenitude, that has its source in the Divine. Inner life becomes sufficient to match outer life. Buddha taught Asia the calm of surrender, Jesus taught the world the calm of conquest.

The one said, "Peace," the other said, "Excelsior." The one was the peace of the reduction of personality, and the other was the peace of a developing, perfecting, adequate personality. Josiah Royce defined faith as "the soul's insight or discovery of some reality, that enables a man to stand anything that can happen to him in the universe." These words echo the New Testament words, "This is the victory that overcometh the world, even your faith." But just as we should not believe in "faith-healing," but Divine healing by faith, so we must not believe that faith heals mental and spiritual suffering, but, rather, that it links us to the resources of the Divine Life that heals us. Nothing now can make us afraid; we are one with that Life. Its purposes are our purposes, its power our power, its safety our safety.

I once said to a student, that no man was safe until he could stand anything that could happen to him. He looked startled and then replied, "Then, not many of us are safe, are we?" Not many, but the Christian, who has learned this secret, is!

The turn came, in one of our Round Table Conferences, for a very noble High Churchman to speak. He was a man in whom we all had confidence, a man of radiant faith and self-sacrifice. This is what he said: "Religion means to me three things: victory, victory, victory." He could not have summed it up better. For the religion of Jesus does mean these three things, victory over sin, victory over self, victory over suffering. It is in the fitness of things that Jesus cried out, "In the world you have tribulation, but be of good cheer; I have overcome the world." This is cheer indeed, a cheer that has faced all the facts of life, good, bad, and indifferent, and has let those facts say their worst, and then in the face of it all bursts into laughter, a joyous, glorious, victorious laughter, a hallelujah chorus out of unhallowed conditions.

There is a bird in India called "the brain-fever bird." In the terribly hot days and nights when the thermometer rises, its shrill notes rise with it. It cries out, "Brain-fever, BRAIN-FEVER, BRAIN-FEVER." It is enough to drive one mad to listen to it. It was on the point of getting on my nerves one day, when I forever overcame it by making it sing a new song, for I interpreted its song as "Hallelujah, HALLELUJAH, HALLELUJAH!" When life shouts to you with its shrill "Brain-fever" notes, we can put them through the victory of our spirit and turn them back as "Hallelujahs."

We sum up the substance of this chapter in the words of another, "We are at home in the universe, and in principle and in the main, feeble and timid creatures as we are, there is nothing anywhere in the world or without that can make us afraid. In other words, we are at peace, at rest. Not that we do not have to fight, but now, the battle itself is the victory. We are certain in our minds. We are convinced of the good, and that it is one with the supreme power."

Very Low Churchman as I am, I use the words of my High Churchman brother as my own: "Religion means to me: VICTORY, VICTORY, VICTORY!"

8

THE CHOICE — RELIGION WITH OR WITHOUT A CROSS

Two periods came in Jesus' life when he was deeply tempted to face the sorrow and sin of the world in a way, other than the one, he took. The one was during the temptation in the wilderness and the other was at the coming of the Greeks. At those two crises there came before him practically all the methods and ways by which men meet these tragic facts of sin and suffering. He rejected them all save one, and through that one became the Light of the World. As we look at these rejected ways, we will recognize many of the ways used, by ancient and modern people, to find a way out of suffering. He knew that they would lead to dead ends, as we are slowly but surely finding out by tragic experience.

At the beginning of Jesus' ministry John the Baptist was calling a nation to repentance. As the thunderous words of the Baptist fell upon the heart of a nation it was moved to repentance. There exists to this day in Mesopotamia a group of people, eight thousand in number, who call themselves "Disciples of John the Baptist." They never became Christians, but are a direct survival of the revival of the Baptist. It must have been a powerful spiritual awakening. People came in a repenting stream to take the baptism of repentance at his hands. Into that line Jesus entered to take that baptism of repentance. The account says that "when all the people were baptized, Jesus also was baptized." He who knew no sin was taking his place in a line of repentant sinners as one of them. It was identification with humanity at the lowest place. He gave up what is hardest of all to give up, namely, one's good name. Before him in the line was probably a harlot, behind him a thief. He seemed one of them, and was counted a sinner.

There must have come a strong reaction against this attitude, for he was inwardly driven into the wilderness to fight it out. He would get away from humanity to see what attitude he should take toward us. What was the issue over which he fought? Was it whether he was the Son of God? I think not. Had he not heard at the baptismal waters, "Thou art my beloved Son"? No, the question seems to have been this. Being the Son of God, would he also be the Son of man, if being the Son of man meant identification with man such as he had taken? To be the Son of man would mean that he would take on himself all that falls on the sons of man. Was that the way? For forty days Jesus deeply brooded and meditated and fought. So deeply was he absorbed, that he forgot about physical hunger. But at the end of the forty days he hungered. He must go back now to feed his weakened body.

"No," said the tempter, "you need not go back. Stay out here. Why go back to men? Feed yourself on miracle, apart. You are the Son of God. That is enough. You need not be the Son of man."

That is the first great temptation of spiritual religion, it is to withdraw, to feed oneself apart, to be exalted by spiritual communion so that the tragedies and pains of life do not touch one, to be a son of

God, to rejoice in that fact, to feed on it. This is the temptation to which mysticism is liable. When religion falls into it, then it becomes an opiate, for, drugged with devotion and wrapped in its exalted states, it puts its devotees to sleep concerning the sin and suffering of the world. It is essentially "an escape mentality." It would solve the problems of sin and suffering by its own isolation. But this will not work. Wherever it is tried, whether in the professor's study of the West, or in the forests of India, or in the convents and monasteries of Christendom, it brings its Nemesis, it inevitably leads to pessimism. The attempt to escape the gloom of the world brings on an inner gloom of spirit. The way out of suffering is not to attempt to escape it. Jesus refused this way.

The attempt to escape the gloom of the world brings on an inner gloom of spirit. The way out of suffering is not to attempt to escape it. Jesus refused this way.

Then the tempter suggested: "If you must go back, if you will be the Son of man, then do not take the attitude you took as you began. Don't stand alongside of man in this humiliating fashion, stand on the pinnacle of the Temple; be exalted, lifted above man. Be the sign and symbol of religion, as you stand and be gazed at, and worshiped; be the chosen of God, honored and respected. In that way you will give prestige and position to the cause of the kingdom of God. God will not let you, the Son of God, stand alongside of degraded man, for even if you throw yourself down, God's angels will bear you back up again. Your place is up there, not down here with these wretched multitudes."

The second temptation is to stand up above, aloof, superior, to look down on the multitudes as they sin and suffer, to see their lives only from afar, for you consider yourself superior to all these things. It is the temptation of the Stoic, the "superior man," the Brahman, the cultivated gentleman, the Pope-attitude of mind that stands lifted on pinnacles of position and birth and belief and class. We descend to man but only as "Lady Bountiful," only to give our blessing and benediction, only to discharge "noblesse oblige," only to show how God specially cares for us in that he sends his angels to carry us back to our exalted positions. We never quite get to people. The fact is that when we adopt this attitude, we feel that we belong above other people, and are not really a part of them. It all meant that Jesus would not be the Son of man. He would escape the sufferings of men by insulation. But this too would be "an escape mentality," however lofty it might seem to be. Jesus rejected it.

Then came the subtle third temptation which was this: "If you are determined to be the Son of man, then be the Son of man; if you are to be one with man, then take his methods and spirit; win by being a hail-fellow-well-met, let nothing be between, merge your spirit as well as your sympathy and interest, go the full way." To fall down and worship Satan meant to take the attitude of those who obey him. This temptation is to use the methods of man in order to gain man, to gain the world and its kingdom by using worldly methods.

But Jesus refused this temptation as well. Jesus would be the Son of man. He would let everything that falls on men fall on him. But there would be this exception, in deepest spirit he would be different. Jesus would be like them and yet unlike them. He would be the Son of man, but he would also be the Son of God. He knew that only as he was inwardly different could he change men. But in everything else he would be like them.

Lawrence of Arabia says that "no man would lead the Arabs except he ate the rank's food, wore their clothes, lived level with them, and yet appeared better in himself." Jesus would take his place alongside of humanity, would meet everything that we meet, would call on no power for his moral and spiritual battle that is not at our disposal, would face life as a real man, and yet would carry within himself something that is different. It is in that "difference" that our hopes lie. For we need someone who is like us to be our Example, but we need someone unlike us to be our Redeemer. If he were only like us, he could be only our Example. If he would be only unlike us, he could be only our Redeemer. But we need both, Example and Redeemer. Jesus in these temptations fought out the question of how to be both, and won.

> *We need someone who is like us to be our Example, but we need someone unlike us to be our Redeemer.*

But he knew that the choice that he had made would mean his ultimate identification with man on the cross. He had been baptized between sinners; he would be crucified between thieves. The problem of sin and suffering could only be met by an honest facing of the problem; there would be no escaping, no subterfuges, no make-believes, no short-cuts, no drugs. It would be solved, not escaped. And, it would be solved by standing with man from within, not by bending over man from without and touching him with tongs as it were.

He then put his feet upon the way that he knew would ultimately lead to a cross.

But there came the moment of another great pull to get him to take another way. It was at the moment of the coming of the Greeks. This incident is largely lost to Christendom. We usually take out of it the text, "Sirs, we would see Jesus," and leave it at that. But this is one of the most fateful moments in the life of Jesus. It is a moment comparable in importance with the wilderness temptation. In many ways, it was more subtle and difficult than the wilderness experience, for the wilderness represents the temptation of the beginning of one's career, but this coming of the Greeks represents the temptation of mid-career. In mid-career there is the temptation to compromise, to let down on sharp insistences, to take an easier way.

At the coming of the Greeks we see into the depths of a great soul crisis. What was it that made him say, "Now is my soul disquieted"? The whole account has in it something far more than we could expect from the mere coming of the Greeks for an interview. Moffatt in his translation rescues the account for us.

> Now there were some Greeks among those who had come up to worship at the festival; they came to Philip of Bethsaida in Galilee and appealed to him, saying, "Sir, we want to see Jesus." Philip went and told Andrew; Andrew and Philip went and told Jesus. And Jesus answered, "The hour has come for the Son of man to be glorified. Truly, truly I tell you, unless a grain of wheat falls into the earth and dies, it remains a single grain; but if it dies, it bears rich fruit. He who loves his life loses it, and he who cares not for his life in this world will preserve it for eternal life. If anyone serves me, let him follow me, and where I am, there shall my servant be also: if anyone serves me, my Father will honor him. My soul is now disquieted. What am I to say? 'Father, save me from this hour'? Nay, it is something else that has brought me to this

> hour: I will say, 'Father, glorify thy name.'" Then came a voice from heaven, "I have glorified it, and will glorify it again." When they heard the sound, the people standing by said it thundered; others said, "An angel spoke to him." Jesus answered, "This voice did not come for my sake, but for yours. Now is this world to be judged; now the Prince of this world will be expelled. But I, when I am lifted up from the earth, will draw all men to myself." (By this he indicated the kind of death he was to die.) (John 12. 20-34).[1]

It is probable that the Greeks came as an embassy to suggest that Jesus leave the Jews and come to the Greeks. This is not farfetched, for tradition tells us that the Prince of Edessa did send an embassy to Jesus, asking him to come to Edessa. These Greeks probably saw the storm that was gathering about his head; they perceived that he would end in disaster if he went on among the Jews, they would kill him. It is probable that they came, therefore, to invite him to get out of the whole situation, to come to Athens, where men's minds were broad and liberal, where the teaching such as Jesus offered would be appreciated, and where he could live long as an honored and respected teacher. Why go to Jerusalem, where disaster awaits? Step out and come to Athens instead.

This is the issue between Athens and Jerusalem: Athens with its bright, surface interest in everything, but sounding no depths, and Jerusalem with its cross. Which way would Religion, as personified in Jesus, go? Would it go to Athens to escape suffering or would it go to Jerusalem to face suffering? It was the battle of the good and the best:

---

1 James Moffatt, *The Holy Bible: A New Translation.* Harper & Brothers, Publishers, New York. Used by permission.

the good without a cross, the best with one. All systems, all men line up on one side or the other of that issue. They will take the Athens method of dealing with sorrow, the method that attempts to explain it, or explain it away by words, by mental suggestions, by Pollyanna views of life, by hypnotisms of ideas, by subterfuges both mental and spiritual, by etherealizing one away from the facts, by soporific; or, they will take the Jerusalem way, the way of going straight toward the worst that life can say or do, the way of letting the storm strike one, the way of accepting Calvary.

Jesus saw the issue very clearly, so we hear him soliloquizing, "Except a grain of wheat fall into the earth and die, it abideth by itself alone; but if it dies, it beareth much fruit." The Greeks had probably suggested that Jesus could live a long and fruitful life among them. Why throw it away now? This was his answer: Life comes through giving of life, fruitfulness through falling into the ground and dying. Jesus would live not by the hourglass, but by the heartbeat. Many of us have chosen the Athens way; we are abiding by ourselves alone, using only human resources, finding life shallow and fruitless; refusing to pay the ultimate price of giving ourselves, we find ourselves paying the price of the deadness of life itself.

Again, we hear Jesus: "He that loveth his life (as these are asking me to do) shall lose it, but he that loseth it (as I see I must do) shall find it again." The Greeks were asking him to love his life and save it, and thus save others; they were asking him to bless without bleeding. But Jesus knew it could not be done.

However, the struggle is great, for this cross that looms before him is no make believe. Again, we hear the inward battle: "Now is my soul disquieted." And well it might be! But some of us are not disquieted at all at this point. We fall in with the spirit of the age which would say, "Accept Athens as opportunity, shun Jerusalem as calamity." So, we accept its spirit and share its shallowness. But a growing number are disquieted at this issue. They have the feeling that if they miss this, they miss life.

Again, we hear Jesus say: "What shall I say? Father, save me from this hour?" Would he ask to be excused, to be let off from paying the supreme price? Some of us are asking just that. We are asking to be saved from this hour. It is true that we still call God "Father" at the very moment of asking to be excused, we are still religious, still holding certain allegiances, but making the supreme refusal of ourselves. We ask to be saved "from," not *for* this hour. But Jesus answers in a decisive way: "Nay, it is something else that has brought me to this hour. All the ages have matched me against this hour, all the yearnings of men and women have brought me face to face with this moment. I cannot fail now, for if I did, I would fail them." It is a great moment in a person's life when he can say "Nay" to all lesser roads, to all easy ways, to all compromises, to all temptations to go to Athens. But it is a greater moment when he can see through the depths of things and realize that there has been "something else," some divine providence that has brought him to this moment, that he is now merging his will with an Almighty Will, and that Will is sacrificially redemptive.

> *Life comes through giving of life, fruitfulness through falling into the ground and dying. Jesus would live not by the hourglass, but by the heartbeat.*

Now we hear the great decision made by Jesus: "I will say, Father, glorify your name. Do not think of what it will cost me, only glorify your name." Jesus gave God a blank check; blank save that it was signed with his own blood. The ages hung on this moment, and he did not fail them. It is life's greatest moment when we hand to God that blank check signed in our own blood, joyfully asking God to call on us for all we have, including ourselves. It is the moment of the Great Renunciation, for him and for us.

However, that is followed by the Great Annunciation. Listen: "After that, came there a voice from heaven, saying, I have both gloried it, and will glorify it again." The moment he made the final response then heaven spoke. Many of us who are living under silent heavens would find them vocal with the voice of God, if we should choose the Jerusalem way. God would speak to us out of the pages of Holy Writ, out of the voice of providence, and within the depths of our own spirits, if we chose his way with a final decisiveness. Life would then take on meaning, purpose, plan.

It was interesting to see how the by-standers took all this. Some said, "It thundered." To them it was just the impersonal voice of nature with no meaning to it. This interpretation is that of materialistic naturalism. When we hear God speaking to us in answer to our supreme dedication, they say, "It thundered." When we go through a soul-transforming crisis, and emerge from it as regenerated beings, they solemnly declare, "Adolescent phenomena, it thundered." When we come home from some group in which we have caught a life-changing vision of Christ, they say, "Mob-psychology, it thundered." When we feel the pain and misery and sin of the world and dedicate ourselves to its healing, they declare, "Gender-manifestation, it thundered." When God's hand is laid on us in physical healing, their reply is, "Mental suggestion, it thundered." When we find ourselves lifted out of ourselves by prayer, and when we rejoice in transformations wrought, we are told, "Auto-suggestion, it thundered." Those are the attitudes and interpretations of one group of bystanders.

There is another group of by-standers with its own interpretation: "An angel spoke to him." To them, it was something more than the voice of nature, and something less than the voice of God; it was the voice of an angel. People of this type are more spiritually inclined, but are not deeply engaged. They are spiritualistic rather than spiritual. They are more interested in "phenomena," in psychic manifestations, in dark rooms rather than in the dark places of sin and need of the earth; in communications from the dead rather than communicating the Good News to the living. The attitude lacks moral depth.

I am not prepared to say that the dead do not speak to the living, I keep an open mind, awaiting further evidence. But even if they do, I do not think that it produces the healthiest type of religion or character to concentrate on getting connection with the dead, especially if it weakens our connection with the problems of the living.

Both groups are "by-standers" – "those that stood by said." Anyone who stands upon the edges of life as a by-stander is bound to give a shallow interpretation to life. It is only those who have faced the alternatives of Jerusalem or Athens, and have chosen Jerusalem, who can really interpret life. *They are in life.* They know what the cross means, for they can feel it cutting into their shoulders; they know what suffering means, for they are being crucified on a cross of a chosen pain. However, they also know what life means, for they feel throbbing, bursting, singing life coursing through every fiber of their beings. They know life from within! They are no by-standers.

As a result of this momentous choice, Jesus saw that three things would happen: First, the judgment of this world. "Now is the judgment of this world." What had the choosing of a cross have to do with the judgment of this world? At first sight, they seem unconnected, but at second glance, we find them intimately connected. The cross is the judgment seat of this world. It is there that men are really judged. I must confess I feel no inward trembling, when I picture God's throne on the last day, but this Man upon the cross judges me, condemns me, and sends me to my knees. Jesus' spirit of facing the world's sin and suffering, makes my spirit tremble within me like an electric needle in a storm. Here at the cross, his love judges my hate, his all-inclusiveness judges my narrowness; his self-sacrifice judges my selfishness. The by-standers had said, "It thundered," and at the moment, that choice of a cross becomes the thunder that reverberates through our guilty spirits and makes us afraid. He was right when he said, "Now is this world to be judged."

Second, the expulsion of the power of evil from this world: "Now is the prince of this world to be expelled." Jesus would expel sin and suffering from the world by taking them into his own heart, and there smothering them to death. Jesus would expel the prince of this world, not by breaking his head, but by letting the prince of this world break his heart. Jesus would expel suffering by taking suffering, would expel sin by becoming sin.

Third, Jesus would manifest supreme power in choosing this cross. "And I, if I be lifted up from the earth (on a cross), will draw all men unto myself." Here was to be manifested a new type of power, the power of overcoming evil with good, hate by love, and the world by a cross. It was the power of turning the other cheek, of going the second mile, of giving the cloak also, of drawing persons in by dying for them.

The choice was made. He would thank the Athens group, but refuse their offer. Jesus would choose the people who were rejecting him. There was no other way, for Jerusalem and the hill called Calvary lay between him and the Easter-morning Victory. He could not teach men to sing who bear crosses, unless he allowed his own voice to be hushed on a cross.

The penetrating words of *How Can I Sing?* – written by an anonymous poet are true:

"I want to sing lyrics, lyrics,
Mad as a brook in spring;
I want to shout the music
Of flushed adventuring.

"But how can I sing lyrics,
I, who have seen today
The stoop of factory women,
And children kept from play?

"And on an open hilltop
Where the cloak of the sky is wide,
Have seen a tree of terror
Where a black man died?

"I want to sing lyrics, lyrics,
But these have hushed my song;
I am mute at the world's great sadness,
And stark at the world's great wrong."

No one can sing lyrics in a world like this unless he has learned "the song of the Lamb," the song that is learned through suffering, through taking the cross to one's heart, putting strings to it and making it into a harp.

But before we can sing that song we must pause and go deeper and try to sound the depths of that cross which Jesus has chosen.

> *Jesus would choose the people who were rejecting him. There was no other way, for Jerusalem and the hill called Calvary lay between him and the Easter-morning Victory.*

9

THE COST TO GOD

When we look at life, it seems to speak two great contradictory words. Nature seems to spell hard, unbending, unforgiving, iron law. On the other hand, religion offers to us forgiveness, restoration, a new chance. Look up through nature to God, and you come to the conclusion that God is Law. Look up through Christ to God, and you come to the conclusion that God is Love. Can these two be reconciled, or must we make our choice between them?

There is no doubt that there are these two sets of facts. The one set of facts has been built up by India into the law of Karma. Reduced to its simplest form, and to its central meaning, the law of Karma means that we reap what we sow. This law insists that this is a moral universe, with moral consequences, that some way, somehow, somewhere you will find again the results of your doing. Inevitably, invariably, irretrievably you meet again what you do. If this is the essence of the law, I can accept it wholeheartedly. This does not mean that by accepting Karma, one has to accept the doctrine of the transmigration of soul, which is a corollary built up around Karma to explain the inequalities of life. Of transmigration, I see no sufficient proof. Of Karma, I am confronted everywhere with the strongest evidence.

You may be free to choose a deed, but you are not free to choose the consequences of that deed. It registers itself in result in our moral natures. It may not be seen to result in outward punishment, but it will inevitably produce deterioration, even where evidence of outward results is lacking. This law is colorblind. If the white man, the black man, the brown man or the yellow man breaks it, it breaks him. It is religion blind. This law does not ask whether you are a Christian, Muslim, Hindu, Buddhist, or agnostic; break it and it will break you. The fact is that we do not break this law, we break ourselves upon it. When we break it, it throws us back a quivering, bleeding, blighted thing. This applies to groups, to nations, to races as well as to individuals. There is a national Karma, as well as an individual Karma. On a small scale and on a large scale the universe sides with good and against evil.

"The sins which you do in two and two,
You must answer one by one."

This makes our universe seem very hard and unforgiving, and yet it burns into our minds the fact that this is a universe of law, and not a universe of whim, fancy and notion. We know what to expect. The discipline of our universe is very strict, but it is dependable. I prefer to have a dependable universe rather than one upon which we could not depend as to which side it would take.

We need not to insist on this further, for the history of mankind is the history of the working out of this law. "All things betray thee, who betrays me," said Francis Thompson in "The Hound of Heaven," and so he simply put into a single sentence what is written in the constitution of things.

Nevertheless, this is not the whole truth about the matter. There is another side, which is seldom looked at in discussing Karma. It is not true that we alone reap what we sow. The results of our deeds are passed on to others, whether for good or for ill. There is such a thing as the law of transference of Karma. Other people reap what we sow. A father in a home sins, and he would probably give anything if he could take all the results on himself, but he cannot. His wife, his children, his friends, and all who live within the circle of love to him feel the result of his doing. Every life is bound up with every other life. There are no isolations, there are no insulations. If I raise my life, everyone else feels the upward pull of it, but if I let my life sag, everyone else feels the sag of it.

If the law of the transference of Karma is true, and I think it is just as deeply rooted a fact as the law of Karma, then it opens up the way for us to think in terms of the vicarious. Thinking of the vicarious transference of "Karma" makes it possible to think in terms of a cross. If there were One who could stand at the center of life and who, by the universality and depth of his love, could gather up into his own heart the sins and sufferings of men, he could transfer to them the results of his own Karma. In that case, men would eat the fruit, not of what they sowed, but of what he sowed. There is at least the possibility of thinking in these terms. We shall explore that possibility.

Before we go into the ideas underlying the cross of Christ, let us look at one or two presuppositions. Rightly or wrongly, as Christians we rightly believe and look on Jesus as the human life of God. Jesus is that part of God which we have been able to see, the uncovering of the Divine. Jesus is the Divine speaking to us in a language we can understand, a human language, showing us his character where our characters are made, namely, in a human environment. We do not see how else God could show himself except in just this way. If that be true, then what fell on Jesus, fell on God, what he bore, God bore; his cross was God's cross. Subsequently, this outward cross that was lifted up in history, is a sign of that inward cross, that lies upon the heart of God. We who are bounded by our senses could not see this inward cross upon God's heart, unless, and until it was lifted up before our senses. The Italian painter was crudely right, then, when he pictured the nails driven into the hands of Jesus, as going through the wood and into the hands of the Father at the back. These conception echoes the statement of Paul when he says, "God was in Christ reconciling the world unto himself."

We cannot separate God and Christ, making one hard and unbending and the other tender and forgiving.

We cannot separate God and Christ, making one hard and unbending and the other tender and forgiving. A little girl said, "I hate God, but I love Jesus, for God was going to destroy the world, but Jesus wouldn't let him." She expressed in a child's outburst, what has been built up into theological systems. But the New Testament unfolds to us the Christ-like God. When Jesus says, "He that has seen me has seen the Father," he means, among other things, that "he that has seen me on the cross has seen the Father on the cross." The cross, then, is God's heartbreak.

That heartbreak is inevitable in a world like this. In a human home where love meets sin in the loved one, at the junction of that love and that sin, a cross of pain is set up. A pure love suffers when it comes into contact with sin in the loved one, and the purer the love the more poignant the pain. When the pure and holy love of God comes into contact with sin in us, his loved ones, then at the junction of that sin and that love a cross is set up. It is inevitable. It is inherent in the nature of things. There is no mechanical transference, but there is a vital acceptance on the part of love. For love cannot be love and remain apart and aloof. If it be love, it will insinuate itself into the sins and sorrows of others and make them its own.

"I do not want to cast my sins on Jesus," said a Swedish lady who had turned Buddhist. "It is degrading to ask another to take your sins."

"I agree," I replied, "but while you would not cast your sins on Jesus, and ask him to bear them, you cannot help his taking them, whether you ask it or not. Since Jesus is Love, he is bound to take them without your asking." Love cannot be love and refuse the burdens of love. In a world like this, God cannot refuse the cross and remain a God of love.

If, therefore, in the midst of our pain and suffering we cry out in protest that God has made a world in which sin and suffering are possible, let us remember, that if it costs us a great deal to live in a world like this, it costs God more to make one like this. To make one like this meant that he had to live in it as Love. That meant his own cross. **God could have made one in which there was no possibility of sin and suffering; but had he done so; he would not have made us as free moral beings, capable of choice.** He could have made us puppets, not persons; machines, not men. God chose, on the contrary, to make the great adventure, and to create moral beings capable of good and of evil. Love could not have done less. A human parent creates a child upon whom he can lavish his love, though in doing so he runs a very great risk of bringing into the world a child who might go astray and break his heart, yet the parent assumes that risk, for love cannot do less. God, the Divine Parent, takes the same risk in creating us, for in the end it may break his heart. It did. The cross is the sign of it. At creation, God assumed a responsibility, and at the cross he acknowledges and discharges that responsibility. He would take on himself all that falls on us, and more! Only on that basis could he create. But on that basis he did create. And it must be that God has something so wonderful in mind in the re-creation, that he took the risk of the creation. That ultimate plan and goal is veiled from us, "We know not what we shall be," but now we see the cross. That holds us. If the revelation of what we see in the cross is true, then we can trust what lies back of it. If the Heart that is back of the universe is like this gentle, strong Heart that broke upon the cross, then God can have my heart, and that without reservation.

But the objection is raised: If God suffers, God is unhappy; if he is unhappy, he is imperfect; if he is imperfect, he isn't God. This objection is based on a fallacy. What is the law of happiness in this universe? It is this: the really happy are those who deliberately take on themselves pain for the sake of others; and the unhappy are those who center on themselves, and refuse to do anything for others at cost to themselves. They become bored and annoyed. The God who would sit apart from the tragedy and pain and misery of the world would be a God, self-centered, therefore unhappy. But the God who would know the joy of a cross, would be a God who would know the deepest joy of this universe, the joy of saving others at cost to oneself. The God who would have the highest thing in the world, namely, love, absent from his nature, would be a God who would be imperfect, and therefore not God. The psalmist asks: "He that planted the ear, shall he not hear? He that formed the eye, shall he not see?" And Browning adds, "He that made love, shall he not love?" And we might add, "He that put the impulse to sacrifice self in the heart of the highest of men, shall he not sacrifice himself?" If there isn't a God like that in the universe, there ought to be one!

If the law of Karma is written within the constitution of things, this law of love is written there as well. If the hillsides are scarred by the roaring torrents, nature sets to work to fill those scarred ravines with flowers to hide the scars. If a bone is broken, the whole body rushes with materials for the healing of that break. If a wound is infected, millions of cells will sacrifice themselves in the battle to throw off the infection. When ants cross a stream, some will make a bridge of the dead bodies of their companions, so that the rest can walk across in safety. The blossoms die that the fruit may come.

> The God who would have the highest thing in the world, namely, love, absent from his nature, would be a God who would be imperfect, and therefore not God.

In South America, I was given some stones taken from the bed of a certain river, which when cut into cross sections, had a clearly defined cross in the center. There was also given to me in that land, a section of a huge grapevine, which had a perfect cross in its heart. The cross is in all life, it is sleeping in the stone, comes to clearer life in the vine, is clearer still in the animal, shines more fully in man, and comes to its fruition and perfection in the cross of Christ. And that cross is the revelation of God. In the beautiful lines of E. M. Plunkett:

I see his blood upon the rose,
And in the stars the glory of his eyes.
His body gleams amid the eternal snows,
His tears drop from the skies.

All pathways by his feet are worn,
His strong heart stirs the ever-beating sea,
His crown of thorns is twined with every thorn,
His cross is every tree.

Someone has said that "life is sensitivity." At the lowest life we find sensitivity at a very low ebb. There is none in the stone. But it is found in the plant, for Professor Bose by his experiments has proved that plant life is capable of responding to affection and hate, and suffers as it dies. But the suffering is small. It is more pronounced in the animal, but not highly developed, for the animal may have a narrow range of affection. It is clearer and fuller in humans; the higher in the scale of character one goes, the more sensitivity we manifest, the wider our range of affection, and hence the greater capacity for suffering. When one comes to the highest life of all, namely, God, we would expect that this sensitivity would be manifested in its perfection. The cross says that it is. The cross is God sensitive to human sin and sorrow, so sensitive that it becomes his very own. Goethe said, "If I were God, this world of sin and suffering would break my heart." Of course, it would. It did!

Jesus manifests this sensitivity supremely. Everything that hurts man hurts him. As Joseph Parker said, "Jesus was never off the cross," never off the cross because man was ever in sin and suffering. Hutton says that F. D. Maurice felt "a sort of self-reproachful complicity, in every sinful tendency of his age." Mencius wrote that the emperor who first dammed the rivers of China said, "I feel personally responsible for every man who drowns in China." The emperor who was called "the Agricultural Emperor" of China said that he felt "personally responsible for every man who starves in China." Jesus goes deeper, and by the breadth of his love, shows that he feels every man's sin and suffering as his very own. Every man's sin is his sin, every man's pain is his pain. This is the meaning of his "bearing our sins in his own body upon the tree." Jesus bore them not mechanically but vitally. They were not laid on him, as they of old laid their sins upon the scapegoat, but he took them as a mother would take the sin of a wayward son into her own heart, and would suffer the shame and penalty with him.

Doctor Coffin tells of a British sergeant on the Somme, who said that throughout the long months the two battle lines kept up their continuous exchange of shells, he could not get away from the feeling that Christ was out there, between the lines, and that the shots passed through his body. On a tablet in the chapel of the Peking Union Medical College, in memory of Doctor Hall, who died of plague infection, while attending to his patients, is written what a Chinese patient said of him: "He took my sickness into his own heart." When the gospel says that Jesus "himself took our infirmities," it means far more than the healing of the infirmities of those around him. He "took" them; they became his very own, every pain his pain. Just as when you touch the sensitive nerve anywhere in the human body, the shock of the contact is felt in the brain, so Jesus as the Head of a sinning, suffering race, feels the ache of it all in his own being.

It was said of a sage in India, that he saw some men beating a water-buffalo, and lo, so sympathetic was he to the poor beast, that the marks of their sticks appeared upon his own back. We see in Christ's wounds, our wounds, in his lashed and bleeding back, the outer sign of the inward lashings of our own guilty consciences, in his rejection, the rejection of our own guilty selves, in his cry of dereliction on the cross, our own cry. He was:

The Nerve o'er which did creep
The else unfelt oppressions of the earth.[1]

A Swami was baptized at our Ashram and became an ardent disciple. He was a lion of a man. He was talking to a group of Hindu lawyers when one of them made a disparaging remark about Jesus' birth, saying with sinister suggestion, that Jesus had been born out of wedlock and, therefore, in sin. The Swami, infuriated, took off his shoe and with it struck the lawyer several blows across the shoulders. The Swami went away in hot indignation, feeling that he had been righteous in defending his Lord. But that night, as he lay thinking about the matter, Christ came to him, and as he stood there without a word, he quietly removed the robe from his shoulder, and there the Swami saw the marks of his own shoe upon the shoulder of his Lord. He saw that his Lord had received upon his own shoulder, the blows he had laid on one of his enemies.

When the Jewish leaders delivered Jesus over to the Romans, the soldiers felt that their opportunity to vent their contempt and hate upon the Jewish race had come. Here was their Jewish "king," they would show what they thought of the Jews, by showing contempt and

---

1 Percy Bysshe Shelly, *Julian and Maddalo: A Conversation* (John and Henry L. Hunt, 1824).

scorn for their "king." They probably had no personal hate against Jesus, but did so for the Jews! So, they vented scorn on their "king." They dressed him in royal robes, pressed a mock scepter in the form of a reed into his hand, put a crown of thorns upon his head, and bowed the knee before him, crying, "Hail, king of the Jews." All this contempt was intended for the Jews, and yet Jesus took what was intended for his crucifiers as his very own and bore it, for them!

It was said of Chaitaniya, the great Bengali devotee, that he was once very cold, so cold that life seemed to be passing away. His frightened disciples wrapped him in all the blankets they could find, but he seemed to be dying of cold in spite of it all. One of the disciples, feeling that there must be some other reason for his master's coldness, began to look around to see if he could find the cause. He found a "chamar," an outcaste man huddled up in the corner, shivering with the cold. "This chamar," said the disciple to himself, "must be the reason why the master is cold." So, he ran off and got blankets and put them on the chamar, and as the poor man began to warm back into life again, Chaitaniya began to grow warm also. This may be only beautiful legend, but it is a glorious fact in Christ. "Inasmuch as you have done it unto one of the least of these my brethren, you have done it unto me." Jesus is cold in the chilled bodies of the poor, he is lonely in the outcaste, is hurt in the guilt of the sinner, and Jesus is part and parcel of every life. What a choice Jesus made when he became the Son of man! The choice meant that he chose all that concerned the sons of man. Sin and suffering concern them chiefly. Christ took them too.

The words of Eugene Debs have in them some echo of the cross: "Years ago I recognized my kinship with all human beings, and I made up my mind that I was not one whit better than the meanest of the earth. I said then, and I say now, that while there is a lower class, I am of it, while there is a criminal class, I am of it, while there is a soul in prison, I am not free."

A government official in India told me how he became a changed man. Everyone could see that he was a changed man, and the story of that change was of interest chiefly because of the wonderful result. He said that he took his first step into immorality when he went to Europe to study. He had left behind him a pure, innocent, trusting wife, the soul of honor. When he came back from Europe instead of turning from his unfaithfulness, he continued his double life. The purity and trust of his wife stabbed him like a knife, until the time came when he could hold the guilty secret no longer. He determined to tell his wife, but he was inwardly afraid she would probably leave him, or wither him with her anger. But one day he decided to face it, so he called her into the room, shut the door, and began to unfold the whole wretched story. As the meaning of what he was saying dawned upon her, she turned as pale as death, staggered against the wall, and leaned there with the tears trickling down her cheeks. As he stood watching he saw his sin crucifying his wife, her pure love was being tortured on the cross of his sin. "That moment," he said, "I saw the meaning of the cross of Christ. I saw from her lesser cross, the meaning of the greater cross. And when she said through her tears that she would not leave me, but would help me back to a new life, I felt the offer of a new beginning in the cross of Christ, and from that

> *Jesus is cold in the chilled bodies of the poor, he is lonely in the outcaste, is hurt in the guilt of the sinner, and Jesus is part and parcel of every life.*

moment I was a new man." Suffering love had redeemed him. It is the only way of redemption.

We began this chapter by the insistence upon the fact of the Law of Karma, the hard, unbending, unforgiving, iron law. But we have seen that this law is not the whole truth. There is the fact of the transference of Karma. If God is Law, he is also Love. Both are there. Their reconciliation is the problem.

We feel that if God is Love, there ought to be forgiveness. Does not God ask us to forgive those who sin against us? Shall he do less than he requires of us? We cannot feel that he will. But we also feel that if there is forgiveness, there can be no cheap forgiveness. Our moral natures would revolt against it, we could not take it. How can law be saved and love be manifested at one and the same time? When two young men were guilty of immorality in the ashram of Mahatma Gandhi, it broke his heart. He had preached purity to India and yet impurity had invaded his own ashram. Out of sheer sorrow of spirit, Gandhi began to fast. For six days he fasted. When after this ordeal those boys stood before Gandhi, and begged to be forgiven and restored to fellowship, could he do it? Yes, he could offer them forgiveness now, for it would no longer be a cheap forgiveness. It had the stain of the blood of his own suffering upon it. If Gandhi as the head of the institution had offered them forgiveness on the basis of that authority, it would have been cheap and easy, and meaningless, as lacking moral quality. If God offers us forgiveness on the basis of the divine omnipotence, then I am sure that we cannot take it. It lacks moral quality. It is cheap. But if he offers us forgiveness on the basis, not of the divine omnipotence, but of the divine self-sacrifice; if God offers it in a nail-pierced hand, then our moral sense will let us take it.

If after the committing of the sin the fellowship is to be restored between the boys and Gandhi, then the latter must take the initiative.

The boys could not say, "Now let us be friends." Their sin stood between them. How could that sin be removed and the fellowship restored? Gandhi had to take the initiative. He had to restore it from his side, by taking the sin on his own heart and letting it break it. When we sin, we cannot get to God, God must come to us. He must restore the fellowship from his side. He must take it on his own heart and must come to us wearing in his own heart our sin and shame and sorrow. The cross is the price that God must pay to get to us in spite of our sins.

The cross, then, is the reconciling place between Karma and forgiveness, between Law and Love. The one upstanding beam of the cross represents the law of Karma, how straight and unbending it stands! The other beam, the wide stretching one, represents the love of God reaching out arms to save and heal. These two, the Law and the Love coming together, make the cross. And the cross makes them one.

In a temple of Peking, one sees the statue of Buddha reciting to us the law of Karma. At the rear, back to back with Buddha, is the Goddess of Mercy. The Chinese felt that they should both be there, but the nearest they could get them was back to back. In the cross they melt into glorious harmony.

Oman says that, first, we must pass through the sense that God and his kingdom are small and oppressed, to the sense that they are triumphant and universal. Second, that we must pass through the sense that God's rule is not even beneficent, to the discovery that it is love. Third, that we must pass through the sense that God's rule is not even just, to the discovery that it is atoning. In the cross, we discover that God's rule is both just and atoning. But I do not see any other place in which we are able to make that discovery.

Here is a son dismissed from college because of drunkenness and immorality. The father could take one of four attitudes: First, "I forgive you—it's all right." Second, "I turn you out, and have nothing more to do with you." Third, "I forgive you, but I will send you away." Fourth, "I will take the boy back into my home, suffer with him and forgive him." That last would be atonement. If God is like that which we see in Christ, we know which way he will take. There was no other way for God to take and remain the kind of God he is. He being what he is, and we being what we are, the cross was inevitable.

All this means, as has been pointed out, that "God does not become loving as a result of human effort to satisfy him. He does not cease to be loving through man's blunder, and sin and failure. That means that grace, and not justice, is the deepest fact about God, and grace is love, spontaneous, uncalculating, going the whole way through, never letting go, never losing patience, and suffering, as one must suffer, when the person who is loved goes wrong."

In the two parables of Jesus, the parable of the pounds and the parable of the talents, there sounds the voice of nature, inexorable, taking away from him that does not use the talent or the pound, to give to those who have much. It is a rigid, unbending, unforgiving demand, that we faithfully develop what we have, or else it will be taken away from us. This is the hard school of selection, the survival of those who are spiritually fit, and who develop their talents. This is the onward march of nature, the upward urge to higher life, but relentless to those who will not relate themselves to that urge.

After giving these parables, the account then says, "When he had thus spoken, he went on before, going up to Jerusalem." At the head of this "upward" procession, is One, who having "thus spoken" these relentless words in the parable and in nature, goes "on before," the goal and guide of this upward movement, giving in himself the key to its understanding. But more than that, he "goes on before" to a sacrificial self-giving at Jerusalem. At the head of the "upward" procession of life, is a thorn-crowned Man, the revelation of what man is to be, and of what God is. The universe finds its consummation in sacrificial love, in a cross. The last word is not to be the inexorable word of the parable that knows no forgiveness, but the last word is seen in the Man himself, and what we see is unquenchable love. The cross finishes the sentence of the parable, and its last word is "LOVE."

> *The crown of life is humanity, the crown of humanity is Christ, the crown of Christ is the cross.*

The crown of life is humanity, the crown of humanity is Christ, the crown of Christ is the cross. As we view the whole of the sweep of nature and of man, we might sum it up in the words of a thoughtful man: "We come then to the inescapable conclusion that progress is growth in love." But we would have never known what love is unless he had "first loved us." The cross is the high peak of that love.

If the law is true that "the extent of the elevation in the scale of existence of an animal or rational being can be infallibly measured by the degree to which sacrificial love for others controls that being," then we feel that we are right in pitching on Christ as the most elevated in the scale of existence; we feel, further, that we are right in bowing the knee at the cross as the highest revelation of that sacrificial love, and that, further still, we are right in taking this as the key that unlocks the mystery of God, and that through a cross we see a God whom we can respect and trust and love. Rufus Jones was right when he said that "Today the most significant aspect which we find for our time in the cross of Christ is its identification with and its revelation of the suffering love of God as Father."

A missionary was interpreting the cross to an audience. A Muslim interrupted, saying: "You don't know what you are doing. You are blaspheming and degrading God when you say that God suffers." The missionary did not answer. A Hindu did: "No," he said, "if we are to believe in any God at all, we must believe in the kind of God that Jesus shows." The Hindu was right. If we cannot believe in this kind of a God, we cannot believe in any kind of a God at all. It is a Christ-like God or nothing. But if we can believe in this kind of a God, then, there is put within our hands a key, a key to the universe and to our own sufferings.

In one of our Round Table Conferences, a sociologist said very thoughtfully, "I believe that the fundamental tendencies of the universe are in Jesus Christ." If this be true, and I believe that it is, then, the central fundamental tendency of the universe is love, and the cross is its illustration and consummation. As Sir Oliver Lodge says: "As we rise in the scale of existence, we find ourselves actually choosing pain and trouble, rather than comfort and ease. The highest kind of pain is voluntary, it is suffered for a cause, or for the sake of others."

At the head of the procession of life, then, is a thorn-crowned Man, his pains healing our pains, his wounds answering our wounds, his love taking our sin.

10

SUFFERING AS A RESULT OF WRONG MORAL CHOICE

In our study we have remarked that suffering comes from within as the result of our own choices, and from without as a result of our connection with environment, which is made up of physical realities and human relationships. We have centered upon the latter, as presenting the most baffling problems, but we cannot overlook the fact that much of our suffering comes from our own wrong wills. Suffering as the result of sin, while easy to be understood, is hardest to be borne. It breaks our inner spirit.

Evil has invaded the whole of the human personality. The evil of the mind is error, the evil of the emotion is suffering, the evil of the will is sin. As the center of the personality is the will, so the center of the problem of evil is sin. Sin is an ugly word, and the modern mind doesn't like it and revolts against it. But it cannot escape its consequences. As Carlyle says, "Sin is, has been, and ever will be the parent of misery."

A very modern person remarked to the writer, with a good deal of satisfaction, that they had gotten "rid of the old-fashioned hell of fire and brimstone." I replied that while to many this may be so, nevertheless, the modern man had found that he was still in the hell of broken law, and that this "new hell" was probably as bad as the old, or worse!

Some months ago, I woke up from a hideous dream in which I had been guilty of an ugly sin. The sense of guilt was terrible, and there was cold perspiration breaking out all over me. But the relief to find that it was only a dream, was too wonderful for words. But sometimes we awaken to find that the sense of guilt upon us, is not a dream, —would that it was! —but it is a stark, stabbing reality.

There is a passage in Kierkegaard's *Entweider-Oder,* in which the seduced, broken-hearted woman writes to the seducer:

> John, I do not say, 'My' John, because I now see, you never were. I am heavily punished for ever letting such an idea be my joy. Yet, yet, mine you are, my seducer, my deceiver, my enemy, my murderer, the spring of my calamity, the grave of my joy, the abyss of my misery. I call you mine, and I am thine-- thy curse forever. Oh, do not think I will put a dagger into you and slay you. But flee where you will, I am yours to the earth's ends, yours. Love a hundred others, but I am yours. I am yours in your last hour. I am yours, yours, yours, your curse.

While this cancer of sin is eating, eating at the vitals of our happiness, there is no use talking of victory over suffering. Until this fact of guilt can be lifted from the soul, and restoration of fellowship with God become a reality, the soul withers and pines within one. For many anxious minutes a little boy, child of one of our missionaries, was lost from his mother in a London crowd. The distracted mother found him at last, leaning up against the leg of a policeman, sobbing as if his heart would break. That night the younger brother, Bobbie, was crying over some trifle, and the little fellow who had been lost that day came up to his mother and said, "Bobbie is crying over that, but wait till he has some real trouble." To be lost, lost from God, to have a sense of estrangement and orphanage of spirit, is real trouble.

A party of people, so the story runs, were standing on the seashore recounting their sorrows and their losses. One told of a ship that had gone down with all on board; another told of a mound on a foreign shore, the grave of a loved one; each one thought his sorrow was the greatest. But at last one spoke up and said with a sigh, "Mine is the greatest loss of all, for a believing heart has gone from me." They all agreed that this was the profoundest sorrow of all. For many, that believing heart has been buried in the grave of some sin. Said an earnest member of one of our Round Table Conferences, "I do not believe in any religion. Life is misery and the grave is the goal." Loss of faith, and life being misery, seemed to be connected. They are connected.

Mary stood at the tomb, weeping, and when she was asked, "Why weepest thou?" she replied, "They have taken away my Lord." That is the only real cause for weeping. When Jesus is gone, then life turns to ashes. At that hour the soul truly weeps.

This, then, is the supreme pain, the pain of broken fellowship with God. How can it be mended? Has the gospel any healing word here for this kind of sorrow? It has! Its very purpose and genius are found at this place. It may be only a coincidence, and yet it truly represents their spirit, that the last words of each of the four Gospels put together are these: "Written" (John), "world" (Matthew), "recover" (Mark), "God" (Luke). The Gospels have been written that the world might recover God. It is the story, not merely of man's search for God, but of God's search for man.

A girl wandered away from her home, was lost in the life of a great city and ended in a house of shame. Her brokenhearted mother heard of what had happened and left her home to seek her daughter. She took some pictures of herself with her and left one in each of the houses of prostitution. The girl came in one day, glanced carelessly at the picture on the mantelpiece, came nearer, turned pale, it was the picture of her own mother, and on it were written the words, "Come home," and signed, "Mother." She fled out of the place and back to her mother's arms.

"The Gospels have been written that the world might recover God. It is the story, not merely of man's search for God, but of God's search for man."

If the life of Jesus means anything, it means that he is the photograph of God set down amid erring, sinning children, and across the whole is written, "Come home." That is all. But that is enough. And that is the meaning of the incarnation. It is just God saying to his children, "Come home." There is a bosom upon which prodigals can weep out their sin and shame, and there find restoration and healing, whether they be prodigals who have wasted lives in evil, or prodigals who have wasted opportunities for good. The gospel offers the Gospel of the Second Chance, the Gospel of a New Beginning. In a shop window was the sign, "No piece of crockery broken beyond repair." Over the whole of the gospel is written, "No life broken beyond repair."

The last word that John Mark leaves in his Gospel is the word, "recover." It was his word. He needed recovery. He left a linen sheet behind him, when he fled at the arrest of Jesus in the garden; he left a controversy behind him, when he turned back at Pamphylia, but in the end, he left a Gospel.

Matthew, when he became a publican, was the man who had sold his national ideals for Roman money, and yet in the end he left the account of the Sermon on the Mount, the highest ideals ever handed to man.

> *If the life of Jesus means anything, it means that he is the photograph of God set down amid erring, sinning children, and across the whole is written, "Come home." That is all.*

John was the man of bad temper, the son of thunder, and yet he leaves behind him the Gospel of love, and a life that illustrated that Gospel of love.

Luke was the man of perhaps no outstanding sin, just the cultured humanist, but with life unlighted, then Christ touches that dull humanism into a flame of love and passion for man.

All four of these writers put together say that their Gospels were written that the world might recover God, and they themselves illustrate the recovery.

But most of us who are called Christian are not burdened with the sense of guilt of overt acts so much as with the sense of heaviness at our inadequacy, our failure to be living and fruitful and contagious. It is not so much the sense of evil done, as of good not done. If it is evil, it is more inward, the evil of the disposition, of the spirit, the evil of pride and envy and jealousy and inward uncleanness of thought, and of love of money and of self. We wear the continual pain of not being inwardly clean. Oft times the cry of the seventh chapter of Romans is our cry, "For that which I do I know not: for not what I would, that do I practice; but what I hate, that I do. . . For I delight in the law of God after the inward man, but I see a different law in my members, warring against the law of my mind, and bringing me into captivity under the law of sin, which is in my members. Oh wretched man that I am! Who shall deliver me out of the body of this death?" Here was the pain of not being good, good in the depths of one's being. What is the root of the failure of this evidently very religious, but badly defeated man?

In the sixth chapter of Romans, the writer is exulting in the vision of a complete spiritual victory in Christ. He speaks of having "died to sin," of having "our old man crucified with Christ," "sin shall no longer have dominion over you," "being made free from sin," this is a very triumphant note; but it fades out into the note of despair and gloom in the seventh chapter. What is the reason? It seems to be this. In the sixth chapter "Christ," or the pronoun for Christ, is used nineteen times. The emphasis is on Christ, on what was done by him as an act in history. But it is objective, outside of one, in history, not within. The victory of the sixth chapter is the victory of a vision, not an actuality, it was in Christ, but not in experience. Then, after this marvelous vision, ensues the miserable failure of the seventh. In this chapter the word "sin," or its pronoun, is used nineteen times. Here the man seems to be fighting out the battle with sin alone, without moral and spiritual reinforcement. The Holy Spirit is not mentioned in this chapter. This is important. It is a lone battle and a bad defeat. Then comes the eighth chapter with its note of triumphant victory, the victory of experience. It was not merely in Christ; it was in the man himself. In this chapter "Holy Spirit," or its pronoun, is used nineteen times. It is only a coincidence perhaps that these are used the same number of times, but it represents an emphasis. The eighth chapter is consistently victorious, because the man there has not merely something beautiful in Christ, but that beautiful and victorious thing has been actualized in him, as he has laid hold of the resources of the Spirit. "Laid hold of the resources of the Spirit?" That is not quite accurate, because this depicts our laying hold of something, when the fact is that the coming of the Spirit is something laying hold of us, and laying hold of us at our deepest depths.

When modern psychology tells us that out of the subconscious rise the really powerful instincts and forces that control life and destiny, we begin to see the necessity of religion holding this inner fortress of the subconscious, if it is going to hold life at all. *The area of the work of the Holy Spirit is chiefly in the subconscious.* Here the Spirit takes hold of the very depths of life and cleanses it in a bath of his own pure life. Now, we do good, because we are good, good in the very depths of our nature because these depths are held by the Supreme Good. By an entire self-surrender, we have let Christ into the center of our being; now, with him holding the sources, life becomes spontaneous, natural, unstrained, victorious.

A large part of Christendom is looking at the victory in Christ depicted in the sixth chapter, it is alluring, inviting. But the tragedy of seeing life as victory and living it as a victim, is the spiritual history of the majority. Theirs is the liturgy of defeat. And they call it Christianity. But it is not fair to call it Christianity until we, by a complete self-surrender and a bold appropriating faith, have moved on into the eighth chapter and have laid hold of the resources found there, and know by experience the meaning of the words, "For the law of the Spirit of life in Christ Jesus made me free from the law of sin and of death." This is Christianity, for this is the Spirit of Christ operative at the deepest depth, the depth of the subconscious.

One of our greatest Indian Christians, Principal Rudra, underwent a deep conversion of spirit when he got hold of the words, "I am the resurrection and the life." And well he might, for these words hold within them two things that meet two of our greatest needs: "I am the resurrection," the coming of new life to defeated, dull spirits; and "I am the life," the power that sustains the new life continually after finding that resurrection. Life and life sustained! These are presages of victory. Someone has said that "Religion appeals to two instinctive cravings, light on the mystery of life and power for the mastery of life." If this be so, then the gospel meets these two cravings, for it comes as light, and it comes as life.

In this eighth chapter of victory there is the ringing verse: "And we know that all things work together for good to them that love God." The writer connects up this inward reinforcement by the Spirit, with the power to lay hold of "all things," calamities, troubles, disappointments; things good, bad, and indifferent, and make them work together for good. The things themselves may not be good, but when they go through our consecrated purposes, they come out. Just as two cogwheels work together to move machinery, so the consecrated will makes even evil work for the furtherance of its purposes.

But these two things; reinforcement within by the Spirit, and the laying hold on our environment and making it work together for good, belong together. They cannot be separated. We cannot lay hold of our environment and make it work together for good, unless we have been laid hold of at the depths by the Spirit. When the Spirit lays hold of us within, then all things within us work together for good, for everything is then controlled by the Divine Will. Coordinated within, we conquer without.

Heal me at the heart and let the world come on!

11

THE ATTITUDE OF SOCIETY MUST BE VICARIOUS

There is a possible danger in the attitude which we have been advocating. The danger is that the attitude may be taken and given a fatal twist, in the direction of social and economic reaction. The social and economic reactionary may take hold of this attitude and preach it, in lieu of doing something to remove the causes of suffering, which bear upon the individual from wrong social and economic systems.

While many of the sufferings that come upon us are not preventable, nevertheless the most of our sufferings are from wrong human systems, and since they are made by man, they can be unmade by man. It must be borne in mind that while evil can be in the individual will, it can also be in the collective will; it can be in the person; it can also be in the system. There are evil systems as well as evil persons.

The gospel would be a very partial message, if it taught the individual how to use his sufferings for higher ends, but left untouched the systems that cause the individual suffering. A part of an intelligence test is to give the subject the task of bailing out water from a tank, while water is still running into it from a faucet. It depicts a very low level of intelligence for the subject to proceed to bail, without first turning off the water. Any tackling of the problem of suffering that does not go to the sources of that suffering, as they are found in evil systems, is lacking in spiritual intelligence. Judged by that simple test much of our Christian work could scarcely pass the intelligence test. We try to bail out suffering from individual lives and leave in full operation systems, which are the direct and positive cause of that individual suffering.

Shall we rescue individual slaves, or shall we strike at the slave system? Shall we pick up individual drunkards and leave the liquor traffic to continue to manufacture drunkards? Shall we rescue the wounded in war, or shall we strike at the war system? Shall we pick up the wounded by Jericho's road, or send someone out to get the thieves? The obvious answer to all these questions is that we should do both. There is no real choice between an individual gospel and a social gospel. If it is to be a whole gospel, it must include both. But most of us are too small to include both. We alternate between a social or an individual emphasis, and do not hold them in a living blend. The power of the Japanese Christian leader, Kagawa, lies in the fact that he has blended these emphases in a living way. He believes that the individual may experience a personal

There is no real choice between an individual gospel and a social gospel. If it is to be a whole gospel, it must include both.

transformation, and that society must undergo that same transformation, before the kingdom of God is an actuality. It is not true, as claimed by many, that all we have to do is to regenerate the individual, and the regenerated individual will necessarily apply the gospel to the social order. The fact is that this does not usually work, unless the content of the social application is put into the teaching concerning individual regeneration.

In our Ashram in India we give the outcaste man who does the cleaning of the latrines a holiday one day a week, and we volunteer to take his place and do his work. It is not easy for the brown Brahmans or the white Brahmans to do this, for it means becoming outcastes in the eyes of the Hindu community. But very few have refused to volunteer. One Brahman convert did fail to volunteer, and when I asked him when he was going to do so he drew a long breath and said, "Well, I'm converted, but I'm not converted that far." There were limitations upon his conversion! But aren't there limitations upon most conversions? Many are emotionally converted, but the conversion does not extend to the will. Many are converted in their wills, as far as those wills apply to the individual life, but the will is not converted to the extent of its being applied to the sum total of human relationships.

This teaching concerning the Christian attitude toward suffering must be converted, as far as the insistence upon changing suffering, producing systems. It is good to tell the African-American that he has produced in the "Negro" spirituals the most triumphant religious music the world has ever seen, because he has set his difficulties to music; but to leave the matter there, and not give ourselves to the doing away with those difficulties, is to make religion an opiate. It is well to say that a triumphant invalid made the factory work lighter as the laborers thought of her morning and evening smile (see, p. 173), but that does not really touch the heart of the problem. Religion must see not merely that the beginning and the close of the day is lighted by the smile of a triumphant soul, but that the conditions and terms under which these men work during the day, are such that the men themselves, can smile, as they face their tasks, for they know they are not being exploited, but are an honorable part of an honorable partnership in the task of production. Religion to be really effective must go on from the invalid's chair where it teaches the helpless to be helpful, and must stand in the center of our factories and there produce justice. Unless it does, it is not really facing the problem of human suffering. It is putting people to sleep in regard to central issues by raising side issues. When one has gone off into irrelevancies the Chinese say, "He's gone up into the horns of a cow." Religion that does not go to the sources of suffering and cure things there, is up in the horns of a cow. It has twisted itself up into dead ends out of relationship to things, far away from the heart beat of human problems.

Religion that does not go to the sources of suffering and cure things there, is up in the horns of a cow.

I once saw a high-caste woman gain merit by drawing water from a well, and fill the water jar of an outcaste woman. The latter had to stand off at a distance until the operation was over, and the high-caste woman had departed; only then could she come and get her jar. The high-caste woman went away with the glow of having done a good deed upon her, but that glow was an opiate. It blinded her to the deep injustice of the whole situation. It allowed her conscientiously to tolerate the inhumanities of caste, by doing a good deed to an outcaste woman. Religion must not merely fill the water jars of the outcaste whether they be industrial or social outcastes, it must open the wells of human privileges equally to all. It must not merely alleviate but it must eliminate wrong. Justice, not charity, is the demand.

But the gospel of Christ would go further than justice. It would insist that we must take the attitude toward suffering that God takes. God's attitude is not merely that of justice; he goes further and is vicarious. God opens to us the possibility of using pain, but he does not sit down and leave it at that. He is at work, vicariously at work, to remove the roots of human suffering. And society must do the same.

But the gospel of Christ would go further than justice. It would insist that we must take the attitude toward suffering that God takes.

As the contacts of God with human society are vicarious, so the contacts of society with the individual must also be vicarious. The suffering of the individual must be looked on and felt as the suffering of the whole. The failure and sin of any one, must be looked on and felt as the failure and sin of the whole. The hunger of any one, must be felt as a biting hunger by everyone. The spirit of the atonement must work its way into all human relationships.

The lack of that spirit is destroying human society. The Chinese have a saying, "It's not on my body," meaning that they are not responsible. A foreign lady saw an irate mother-in-law dragging her young daughter-in-law to the brink of the river to throw her in. She appealed to the watching crowd to save the girl, but they turned to her in surprise and said, "It's not on my body." It is this lack of the sense of corporate responsibility, that is laying its destroying hand upon China. I was in a city, the streets of which were unspeakably filthy. A Chinese gentleman told me that an encyclopedia reported that this city was the dirtiest city in the world. I turned to this Chinese friend and said to him, "I don't understand this; these shops and stores are beautifully clean, Chinese gentlemen in them are dressed in silk, but these narrow streets are unspeakably dirty."

"It is easy to understand," he replied, "for the shops and stores belong to these men, but the streets don't belong to anybody." So, they all wallowed in corporate filth, because of a lack of corporate responsibility. To say, "It is not on my body," turned out to mean that the results of it were on everybody's body.

The Brahman of India has said concerning the outcaste in his filth and ignorance and degradation, "It's not on my body," as he raised himself in holy aloofness, only to find that when he wanted self-government and freedom for himself, he couldn't get it because the outcaste hung about the body of society like a corpse. If we do not take the attitude of vicarious suffering toward the weaker members of human society, then we will have to take the fact of suffering in ourselves without its being vicarious. It comes back upon us as suffering, unlighted and deadly.

In 1887 Delyonov, as minister of education in Russia and as the representative of the ruling classes, announced that "the children of coachmen, servants, cooks, laundresses, small shopkeepers, and such like people should not be encouraged to rise above the sphere in which they were born." The ruling classes said that the education and uplift of the masses were not their responsibility. "It's not on my body," they said, only to find that in the course of a few swift years, the children of those "coachmen, servants, cooks, laundresses, small shopkeepers, and such like people" were standing on the prostate body of that fallen ruling class. Those who would not accept the hurt of society as their own hurt, had to accept the heel of society upon their necks in a more deadly hurt.

An employer of the West, in callous disregard of the human element in industry, greedily put in every improvement in machinery that promised to increase his dividends and overcome his competitors, even if it did throw millions out of employment. "It's not on my body," he said, as he eliminated men and put in machines, only to find that there was no one to buy his piled-up goods, so his structure came down upon him in a crash. It was and is on his body, disastrously so.

The white man of America has gathered his garments around him as he moved to the outskirts of the cities, in careless disregard of what happened to the African-Americans, as they festered in tenements, and wallowed in social degradation and ostracism. "It's not on my body," he said, only to find that the very degradation of the African-American had degraded the American people in the eyes of the rest of the world. "There is only one way to keep a man down in the gutter, and that is to stay down with him," said Booker T. Washington. In the degrading of that person, we degrade ourselves. The only way to lift yourself, is to lift everyone in sight. In the lifting of others, you yourself grow tall. The white man who says that the condition of the African-American "isn't on my body," will find in the end, that the very degradation of the African-American creates the opportunity for men to manipulate them in their ignorance, to use them for political purposes, and thereby pull down the sum total of society. If it isn't on our body vicariously, it will be there as unproductive suffering.

"It's to our interest that China and Japan should not unite," said a

European military officer to me one day. "Their unity is not on my body," he said, only to find that this lack of unity was paralyzing the trade of his nation in the East, and was making the whole situation so tense that larger and larger armaments had to be piled up on the backs of his groaning nation, creating the possibility of an outbreak there, that would involve many nations, including his own, in a common ruin.

Jesus proclaimed a new kind of order in human society in which every human being would feel himself a part of every other person, in which the suffering of any would be the suffering of all, in which love should be the motivating and sensitizing element back of it all. Paul visualized a new brotherhood, a "body" in which when one member suffered, all members would suffer with it. Just as in a human body, when one part suffers a hurt, the white blood cells from all parts of the body are rushed with their healing and their help, so the health of the whole body of society should be at the disposal of the weakest to heal and to lift.

Jesus proclaimed a new kind of order in human society in which every human being would feel himself a part of every other person...

Jesus represents that new society in himself. Every man's pain and sin were on his body. He felt it all so deeply, that it broke that body on a cross. But that broken body becomes the life of a race. "This is my body which was broken for you," he says as he offers to us his body, which is the outer symbol of a life that felt all, and healed all. Into his body have gone all the suffering and sin and pain of a race, and he transmutes it all and gives it back as the health of the race.

We must not, therefore, twist this glorious possibility of the use of suffering into a religious but really deadly indifference to the suffering of the individual. A wealthy farmer prayed in his family circle that his unfortunate neighbor might not starve. When they arose from their knees, his little girl said to him, "Daddy, you needn't have bothered God with that, for you can quite easily keep them from starving." She was right. Society must not allow religiosity to be in lieu of righteousness. And if it is to be really Christian, it must not stop at righteousness; it must go on to atonement, and make every man's hurt its own hurt, and every man's sin its own sin. And it must remove the causes no matter the cost to itself. It must do this or abdicate as Christian.

12

COMFORT OR CHARACTER?

After Jesus had been with his disciples for nearly three years, during which time they had watched him and had caught his ideas and his spirit, he turned to them and said, "Now you are clean through the word which I have spoken unto you." Through the words that he had been speaking unto them they were being cleansed as individuals, and yet more, for he was cleansing their total conception of life. He was cleansing their universe itself.

Jesus cleansed their idea of God. Many old ideas had been lingering as an incubus, but now before them and with them and in them was the one loving, Heavenly Father of all humanity. He cleansed their conception of humanity, so that no longer were there any high and low, any white or black, any base or noble born, but just one humanity, a human family with God as Father and all men and women as brothers and sisters. Jesus cleansed life: it was no longer something to be escaped; it was good, and they were to have more of it. He cleansed the physical; it was no longer the enemy of the spiritual, but by its dedication to spiritual ends it could become the agent of the spiritual, therefore in itself, spiritual and sacred. Jesus cleansed this world, it was no longer something to be hastened through, but it was to be the scene of the kingdom of God on earth. He cleansed the home, cutting from it all polygamy, all concubinage, and founding it upon the equal worth of one man and one woman in a life-partnership until death parted them. Jesus cleansed religion: it was no longer a set of magic superstitions, but a means of laying hold of divine resources for victorious moral living. He cleansed greatness: it was no longer to be seen in wealth and in power over the lives of men, but the greatest among them was to be the servant of all, and the servant of all was to be the greatest among them. Jesus cleansed power; it was no longer to be seen as military might, it was the power to overcome evil with good, hate by love, and the world by a cross of suffering for the world.

Jesus cleansed suffering! It was no longer a sign of our being caught in the wheel of existence, as Buddha suggests; no longer the result of our evil deeds of a previous birth, as our Hindu friends tell us; no longer the sign of the displeasure of God, as many of all ages and of all religions have suggested; no longer something to be stoically and doggedly borne. It is more than that. *Suffering is the gift of God.*

Only the gospel dares say that, for it is only the gospel that dares say that God too suffers. Moreover, it dares say that this suffering in God is not marginal and accidental, but inherent in the very nature of God as love. It says it because the cross lights up the nature of God. It says it because, as Von Hugel wrote, "Suffering is the purest form of activity, perhaps the only pure form of activity;" and we cannot deny to God that purest form of activity. It says it because it means something, yes, everything, to know that though living in this kind of a world is costing us pain, it is costing God more. But the gospel says all this, because it does not just say it and then leave it there, but shows a way out by its offer of the possibility of the use of pain. The gospel is the most pessimistic of outlooks on life, for it looks at life through a cross, but it is the most optimistic because it believes that that very cross in him and in us can be, and is, redemptive.

The gospel is the only way of life that dares take hold of the nettle of life, dares grasp it firmly where that nettle is sharpest, and then opens its hand and shows flowers there—the very Rose of Sharon itself. I once listened to a row of blind children as they stood and sang, "Our God is a God of love." How dared those blind children sing that? They couldn't if the gospel had not the cross as its foundation and that cross as the revelation of the nature of God.

> *Jesus cleansed suffering! It was no longer ... the result of our evil deeds of a previous birth, as our Hindu friends tell us; ... no longer something to be stoically and doggedly borne ... Suffering is the gift of God.*

The gospel is the only faith that dares say to its followers, "Behold, I send you forth as sheep in the midst of wolves," you will have as much chance of escaping pain from men and from nature as sheep have in the midst of wolves. It could say that because it was also going to say, "I saw the Lamb upon the throne;" and his being on the throne is a pledge that we too somehow, some way, some time, shall pass out of the midst of the wolves of men and of nature, to victory over both.

Think of the audacity of the account that tells us that the Master rode into his triumph on an ass! Rode into triumph, on the symbol of the deepest humiliation! But that is exactly what he did. To men of that day, humility, meekness, love, self-sacrifice, and a cross were asinine. But Jesus rode on the back of them into his triumph. Men are just now awakening to the fact that these are the fundamental foundations of the universe, that everything else is weakness, so that the kingdom of Jesus is "the kingdom prepared from the foundation of the world." His kingdom is written in the very nature and constitution of things.

Someone has said that "there is a serene Providence that rules the fate of nations, that takes no account of disaster, conquers alike by what is called defeat and what is called victory, that thrusts aside enemy and obstruction, crushes everything immoral as inhuman, and secures the ultimate triumph of the best, by the suppression of everything that resists the moral laws of the universe." There is a ring of truth in these words except where they say "a serene Providence." There is hardly at the head of the universe "a serene Providence" unaffected by the pain and struggle of it all. Rather we think of a serene Love that provided for itself, in making a world like this, its own cross.

> *The gospel is the most pessimistic of outlooks on life, for it looks at life through a cross, but it is the most optimistic because it believes that that very cross in him and in us can be, and is, redemptive.*

Portions of Hungary were given over in the Peace Treaty of Versailles to other countries, the dismemberment of a land. There are maps up everywhere with these portions in black, and a crown of thorns upon them. When God, in creating, looked upon the world, he must have seen portions shaded with the darkness of suffering and sin. He must also have seen the crown of thorns upon it all, and that crown was his own. But that crown of thorns is dearer to the heart of the world than all the tinseled crowns of golden might. The book of Revelation speaks of those who wore "crowns as it were"; they were not real crowns, they were only "as it were," but this crown of thorns is the symbol of the deepest reality of the universe, and some day we shall crown Him Lord of all with that. That crown of thorns is the pledge and the promise that the shaded portions shall be redeemed,

> That all the rages of the ages
> Shall be canceled.

We feel, therefore, that we have a solid foundation for our joy. We see that the universe which in the beginning appeared not even to be just, now turns out to be atoning. We see that the universe had to be hard. But it is not "a vale of tears"; rather, it is "a vale of character making"; and character cannot be made except in the strain and stress and struggle. We cannot cry out and say, "Why have you made me thus?" for God hasn't "made" us yet, he is only in the process. If that process seems without purpose, let us remember that if the cross reveals God, there must be a glorious purpose behind it all, for he is willing to pay the supreme price to bring it to pass. I once saw some rug weavers of North India patiently sit week after week and month after month, making one rug. As I stood and gazed at the rug, I felt the futility of sitting there so long, for the rug seemed to be full of blotches and blurs and knots. But I was looking at the wrong side of the rug. When I came around to the weaver's side, I saw the pattern that was unfolding-and how beautiful it was! It was worth the patience. We now see the wrong side of God's purposes, and they seem without pattern as he weaves through the ages. But one day we shall stand and see things as he sees them, and then we will gasp at the wonder of the plan that unfolds. Now we see the blotches and the blurs and the knots, but we also see the cross. That holds us steady. God means well, and he means to make us well.

Jesus said to his disciples, "Let not your heart be troubled," not because they were to be protected from all troubles, but because they were "to believe in God." Faith in God and his redemptive purposes will not save you from the troubles, but will save you through them, for the troubles themselves can be made into the agents of redemption. If this be so, then "even if the world falls to wreck, the man of faith will be undismayed under its ruins." For the fact is that if the worst comes to the worst, we can get along without the world, for we have our own inner worlds. Someone rushed into Mr. Emerson's presence one day and said in a dismayed tone, "Mr. Emerson, they tell me that the world is coming to an end."

Faith in God and his redemptive purposes will not save you from the troubles, but will save you through them, for the troubles themselves can be made into the agents of redemption.

"Never mind," replied Emerson, "we can get along without it."

The man who is not dependent on anything in heaven or earth, except his right relationship with God, is safe. Holding that intact, everything else will swing back. As Jesus hung on his cross, they tore from him everything, everything except the two words, "My God." He held to them; nothing could tear them from his lips or from his heart; and, holding on to them, he swings back again and out of that one phrase rescued from the ruins, builds an eternal kingdom. When Stephen Colonna was driven out of Rome in the 12th century and all his palaces and strongholds destroyed, he was later found on the road and, when recognized, was taunted with these words, "Where are your strongholds now?" To which Stephen Colonna quietly replied, "Here," grasping his heart. That strong-hold intact, everything else can be taken up into one's purposes and life rebuilt out of its ruins.

God seldom uses any person unless he puts that individual through the testing of pain. Jesus begins his ministry with a wilderness experience, but it ends with an Easter morning. Our lesser ministries too need the testing of suffering. When I was called to the ministry, I had money to go to college to study, but it was all swept away by calamity, as the support of the family thrown on me, and the way to fulfill that call to the mission was blocked. I was called, and the way was immediately blocked! But that year spent behind barricades was one of the very best. Knowing poverty by experience, it fitted me to understand the poverty of India. Take out that year, and life's music would be thin, lacking the rich note of suffering. The Malayalee people of South India have a proverb which says, "He who is born in the fire will not fade in the sun." If God, therefore, lets us be born in the fire of adversity and difficulty, depend on it, he is only making sure that we will not fade in the sun of smaller difficulties incident to human living.

I worked for years on notes in a New Testament, hoping that they would be the basis of a book. When, one day, that New Testament was stolen, it seemed that my work of years had crashed. To begin over again to make new notes, was a heart-breaking task! But I had to do it, and now I find that it was the best thing that could have happened to me. I had to go to the whole New Testament afresh. Had the notes I had accumulated for years been on the wide margins, I should have read them, but now I was compelled to find something new. And I did! My New Testament is richer, and so am I, for having lost the old notes. God never takes a thing from our hands without putting something better in its place.

I am convinced, therefore, that "there is a budding morrow in every midnight." Or, as Clement of Alexandria put it, "Christ has turned all our sunsets to sunrises." We have, therefore, often to be like the night bird singing in the night of the coming dawn when there is nothing but darkness around us. But we sing of the Dawn, because we have the Dawn. Christ is our Dawn.

> *God never takes a thing from our hands without putting something better in its place.*

When the disciples of Jesus were on the mount "there came a cloud and overshadowed them, and they feared as they entered into the cloud." But a voice spoke out of that cloud saying, "This is my beloved Son, you must hear him." And they lifted up their eyes and saw no man save Jesus only. That cloud had cleared their vision! Before it came, they were divided in their allegiance, wanting to hold Moses and Elias and Jesus on an equal footing. But after the cloud had passed, Jesus filled their horizon. When clouds come upon our spirits, we must listen, for God will speak. That Voice will speak in that hour, as it cannot at any other time, for the cloud shuts out all things else and shuts us in with God.

We have been dividing our allegiance with other things, good things perhaps—were not Moses and Elias both good men? But we have been tolerating things that cut into our central allegiance and divide Jesus' supremacy. Then the cloud comes down and we fear as we enter the cloud. A rich and cultured lady stood by the graveside of her only child, desolate and wrapped in a cloud of loneliness and sorrow as dark as night. But as she stood by that graveside the voice of God quietly spoke to her. She went from that graveside, to give herself to the care of children of unmarried mothers. She is one of the happiest women in the world now, for in that dark hour the voice of God let her see that she had been dividing her central allegiance with personal interests, and when she lifted up her tear-dimmed eyes she saw no man save Jesus only. Then, she blessed the cloud that cleared her vision.

A very able and gracious lady was stricken with arthritis. Her work in various fields of activity was ended. She lay a helpless invalid, and in great pain for many years. But to say that her work was ended is not quite true. It assumed a higher form. She had them carry her to the window where the factory men went by, going to and from the factory. As they went to their toil each morning, they were greeted with her friendly smile, and at eventide when the day's work was done, there was the same friendly smile. Many a man's toil was lightened by the picture of that beautiful face with its smile— in spite of. For years that face lighted their gloom. When she died, four factories closed down to let the men attend the funeral of the woman who had let them see into the heart of beauty, through the door of pain and who had let them see God through calamity.

No wonder that another sufferer with arthritis, a woman stricken in the very heyday of life and made an invalid for the balance of her days, could tell her pastor, "I would not exchange the wonder and glory of this fellowship with Christ which I have learned through my suffering. This suffering has brought me life." The cloud had cleared her vision.

Two missionaries lost their only daughter from leprosy. "This is the outcome of our service to India," they might have said in their bitterness of grief. But they did not. They came back to India determined to do something for lepers who are suffering as their daughter suffered. They established the Purulia Leper Asylum, which has grown into one of the largest and best facility for the care of persons with leprosy in the world. That daughter did not die in vain, for by her death she opened a home for thousands of her fellow sufferers. The cloud that came over that home in the death of the daughter, cleared the vision of the parents and let them see a human need, which they would not have seen had it not touched them directly.

A friend of mine, an Indian of lovely character and keenness of spirit, told me that he was a proud, aloof Brahmin even after he became a Christian. He felt himself better than others because of his birth. He had no interest in others; he was interested in the fact of his own superiority. Then, one day in a crowded motor bus, he and others were suddenly thrown over an embankment as the bus overturned. He and the rest were in a common calamity. As he crawled out of the wreckage something happened within him, for he saw in a flash, that he was bound up with every other human life and shared their common woes. He came out of that wreck a brother to every man and has lived it since. A Brahmin perished that day and a brother was born. "But," he said with a smile, "it took a wreck to remake me." A cloud of calamity came over them all, and out of that cloud the Voice spoke. Ever afterward, Jesus filled his horizon.

A lady in India who lived as an invalid, walking with crutches because of a spinal affliction, fell down the steps one day, breaking one crutch as she fell, and losing the other on the way. She lay at the bottom of the steps and called for help. But it was noon and the servants were all away. Finally, when no help was forthcoming, with a prayer, she drew herself by the banister, got to her feet after a great struggle, began to walk, and has been walking ever since, without the crutches! The best thing that ever happened to her was that fall, though for the moment it seemed calamity on calamity. But out of the cloud came the Voice that said, "Rise up and walk."

I once ran out of a burning building, the house of one of the saints of the earth. My losses were small, hers were great, almost everything, in fact. As I looked back into the building, out of which we had rescued a few things from the lower floor, I saw a motto against the wall in the hallway with the words, "Rest in the Lord." The flames had formed for a moment, a framework of fire around the words. That motto was the last thing I saw in the burning building; then it too perished in the flames. Perished in the flames? It and the fact that it represented were the only things we really rescued. As we walked away from the ruin, I told the saintly lady that the last thing I saw in the house was the motto with its fiery frame, saying, "Rest in the Lord." She turned to me with a smile that was nothing less than heavenly and said, "That is what I am doing." The house had gone into ashes, but out of it all a smile had been rescued, that told of a heart at rest, and the possession of that smile and that heart, was worth more than all the possessions that perished that day. She said that she was resting in the Lord. She was, but that sounds very passive. I saw something more; she was snatching out of the heart of that calamity a victory of spirit, that made me feel that flames that burn up one's possessions are not a loss, if they could light up a face like that. "Now I begin to be a disciple," said Ignatius, as he went joyfully to Rome to be torn to pieces for the name of the Lord Jesus. "Now I begin to live," said the smile on that lady's face, as her home went to ashes.

13

THE LAST WORD: With Life or With Death?

As Jesus was going to heed the call of a distracted father to come and heal his little daughter, he was interrupted by a woman in deep need. He stopped to respond to her touch of faith, but the incident took time, and word came from the house of Jairus saying that the daughter had died and there was no need to trouble the Master any further. One can see the trembling lips of the father as the dread news fell on his ears. But the account says, "Jesus, not heeding the word spoken, said to the ruler of the synagogue, 'Fear not, only believe.'"

"Jesus, not heeding the word spoken!" But the word spoken was a fact. It was a firsthand fact, straight out of the death chamber. Yet Jesus refused to heed a fact. Why? Well, he was listening to another, and a higher set of facts. This higher set of facts was that spiritual kingdom which Jesus felt was the supreme and ultimate reality. This higher kingdom of spiritual reality was pressing upon, modifying, breaking into and transforming the lower kingdom of physical fact.

Jesus felt that the last word was with that higher kingdom. The lower set of facts said, "The child is dead;" the higher set said, "The child can live." Jesus refused to listen to the word spoken by Death because he was listening to the word spoken by Life.

We live in a scientific age. Science turns away from tradition, from untested hypothesis, to the facts. It is great gain to religion to live in an age that demands facts. This demand for the facts clears away superstitions, makes for reality, and forces religion to stand with its feet upon the ground, and verify itself in the realm of proved reality. This is gain. But while there are gains, there are losses too. We begin to heed the facts so thoroughly that we become a part of them, we cannot rise above them. We become of such a piece with them that we come under their tyranny.

We come to that frame of mind that is non-expectant of anything beyond the physical facts and laws around those facts. The spirit of expectancy, an expectancy that reaches beyond the immediate physical facts, which is so inherent in living religion, fades out. There is little or no sense of miracle, either physical or spiritual. We become so naturalized to our environment, that our religion becomes a naturalism. It is regular, but dull and calculable. There are no surprises in it and no surprises come out of it. We listen to the word spoken; the word spoken by physical facts.

Every man needs reconversion at forty years of age on general principles! Because at forty, we settle down, begin to lose that sense of spiritual expectancy, begin to take on "protective resemblance" to the environment, and play for safety. I once heard an Anglican bishop say, that the period of the greatest number of spiritual casualties is between forty and fifty, and not between twenty and thirty, as one would expect. Why? Well, if "heaven lies about us in our infancy," the world lies about us in our middle age. We come under its standards, fit into its facts, and are slowly de-Christianized.

Jesus entrusted us with the most astounding task ever given to a set of human beings. The task was nothing less than the replacing of the whole present world order, founded as it is on greed, exploitation, and unbrotherliness, with a new order founded on love, sharing, and brotherhood. That new order is the kingdom of God on earth. Obviously, to think of replacing the whole present world order in every single component, economic, social, political, is a breathtaking task. It is breathtaking, when we remember that it includes particularly, the inner motives and instincts, the very texture of spirit, and the minutest inner outlook. The program of the coming of the kingdom of God on earth makes the program of Communism seem simple and conservative.

Jesus entrusted us with the most astounding task ever given to a set of human beings. The task was nothing less than the replacing of the whole present world order, founded as it is on greed, exploitation, and unbrotherliness, with a new order founded on love, sharing, and brotherhood.

Communism deals largely with redistribution in the realm of the economic; the kingdom of God deals with the sum total of life both without and within. If this be true, then, obviously, the central characteristic of a Christian must be daring faith. She cannot fit into things as they are, for she feels that things as they are constitute something less and something other than Christ's kingdom, and to her the supreme reality is that higher set of facts. Jesus made the "kingdom of God" and "life" synonymous. Jesus speaks of entering into "the kingdom of God" and entering into "life" as the same thing. To him the kingdom of God was life, real life, the only real life. That to him, was the supreme word spoken, so that any word spoken on a lower level was not ultimate or final. Therefore, when the word spoken on the lower level was death, Jesus refused to heed it. He knew that the last word was with Life. We have been insisting in these pages that in dealing with the three tragic facts of sin, suffering, and death there must be no subterfuges, no dodging, no mental running away from reality; there must be a stark realism in dealing with them. But, having insisted on this, we are now in a position to say that, while these three things are real, they are relatively unreal. They are intruders. They are not rooted in the ultimate facts of the universe. The ultimately real is not sin but goodness, not suffering but health and joy, not death but life. Sin, suffering, and death are negatives; goodness, joy, and life are positives. The first three are a trinity of denials, the last three are a trinity of affirmations. The future, then, lies with affirmations, no matter what the present word spoken may say. We believe that sin, suffering, and death will be banished from the universe, with the ultimate triumph of the kingdom of God.

Now, from these premises it would seem that if the facts of sin, suffering, and death are not ultimately real, then the way to get rid of them is simply to deny that they exist, change your mind and they are gone. This is to slip into an easy fallacy. It is a denial of the very breath and atmosphere of the New Testament. Look into the face of Jesus as he goes toward Jerusalem to enter into the final struggle with these three grim facts, and see if you can discover there, that he is merely trying to get men to change their minds. No, he knew that these facts were rooted deeper than the mind, they had taken hold of the very instincts of our nature, had become part of us, and their hold could not be broken lightly. It would mean the ultimate price. Sin could not be banished unless he took it on himself and became sin; suffering could not be done away with unless he took it all into his own heart and let it break it; death could not be wiped out unless he himself died. Died and arose! The whole thing must be met fairly and squarely and without subterfuge, met and conquered. In the cross, he met them all, there are signs about the cross of a cosmic struggle; and in the resurrection he conquered them all. There are signs of a cosmic victory about this Easter morning.

> *The ultimately real is not sin but goodness, not suffering but health and joy, not death but life. Sin, suffering, and death are negatives; goodness, joy, and life are positives.*

The account does not say that Jesus did not believe the word spoken about the death of the child. He simply did not heed it. The spoken word was a fact as far as it went, but it wasn't the last word. The last word lay with Life. When we face these three facts, sin, suffering, and death, we do not deny them as facts: we deny them as ultimate facts, and we face them, since he faced them, and conquer them, since he conquered them.

We do not mentally deal with sorrow; we actively deal with it. We take it up and make it subserve and serve the higher realities. We take captivity captive. Professor James says that "this active dealing with sorrow puts a new dimension to life." It does! When the way is blocked in every direction, there is always this possibility of a movement in the direction of the upward. When the "outlook" isn't good, we can always try the "up look." When one has learned this secret, he is no longer bound by the tyranny of the word spoken on this level of the lower; he hears that higher word spoken, takes hold of it as the sinking Peter took hold of the hand of Jesus, and walks upon the raging seas of circumstance and suffering into which men sink and succumb.

Let us look at the four things which men and women fear most: criticism, material insecurity, old age, death.

First, criticism. We fear criticism because it strikes at our self-love. According to the psychoanalyst Alfred Adler, criticism wounds our ego, and since this strikes at the citadel, we resent it. What is the Christian way to meet criticism? It would seem to be this. First, ask the question, is this criticism true? If it is true, then I will correct the thing criticized. I am a better man because of this correction, and therefore because of this criticism. My critics, therefore, become the unpaid watchmen of my soul. It is important that we take this attitude, for the way of meeting life which we are advocating is liable to a twist at this point. We are liable to think that, since we can use injustice toward us, every painful criticism that comes upon us is necessarily an injustice. It may be that the criticism is very just and very much needed. But suppose the criticism is unjust and untrue, are we meekly to bear it? No, we are to take it up into the plan of our lives and use it. Jesus was crucified on misquotations and twisted meanings. He did not merely bear them; he took them all up into his purpose and through these lies spelled out the truth of God. Those misquotations sent him to a cross, but the world now reads through that cross, the truth about God and life. Someone has said that "thinking is just a rearranging of our prejudices." To be a

Christian is to rearrange our unjust criticisms, and to turn them back to the world as an entirely different message.

Before a large audience, a questioner accused the lecturer of being a liar. This happened in a land where "to lose face" is the supreme loss. The lecturer had lost "face" before that great crowd. But only for a moment. He regained "face," and more, by smiling, by showing no resentment, and by dealing with the question at issue patiently and fairly. The incident seemingly passed by. But that night, one of the members of that audience could not sleep. The patience and good humor with which the lecturer had dealt with the matter haunted him. He had his own quarrel with another, and a wrong was rankling in his own heart. For hours he tossed on his bed, until at four o'clock in the morning, after a desperate struggle, he went to the home of his enemy, aroused him, talked over the whole matter, asked forgiveness, received it and gave it. As he went home, day was dawning, in more ways than one! He stood up in the church that morning and asked those whom he had sinned against with his tongue to forgive him. The response was immediate and contagious. Others began to feel the contagion of penitence and good will. Thirty-four quarrels were settled that morning. The whole spirit of the church was changed. The whole thing turned on the axis of the inner spirit by which he met it. Just as the lily lays hold of the muck and slime and takes it up into its own life, transforms it, transfigures it

To be a Christian is to rearrange our unjust criticisms, and to turn them back to the world as an entirely different message.

and presents it to the world as the symbol of purity, so we can lay hold of unjust criticism, born out of the muck and mire of men's prejudices and passions, and turn it into the white truth of God. It is said that "truth can be flashed out in a single blow," true, and it can also be flashed out in a single blow received, flashed out by an attitude of spirit that reveals more of truth and beauty in a moment than all the arguments of the ages. "What is truth?" asked Pilate, expecting an answer in argument and definition, but the world sees it in the spirit of the Man standing before him. The truth was being flashed out at every blow that Jesus received.

So, whether criticism be true or untrue, we can use it and make it the servant of our higher purposes.

Second, material insecurity. There are two ways that we try to meet material insecurity. One is by laying up as much as possible and thus hoping to provide defenses in this way. This method has obvious disadvantages because it brings anxiety and often corrosion of spirit in the accumulation, and, besides, we find, as in the present crash of stock market, that securities aren't secure. The second way, is to renounce the material entirely, to look on it as a bondage, and to extricate oneself from it by complete renunciation. In this way, we try to get rid of the difficulties of the material by washing our hands of it entirely. In each case, there seems to be a bondage: one is a bondage to riches, the other is a bondage to poverty. In either case there is no freedom. You are only free as you are free to use poverty or plenty. The man who is free to use plenty only, is bound by that very plenty; the man who is free to use poverty only, is bound by that very poverty. They are both bound. But the man who, like Paul, has "learned both to abound and to be in want," is free. Gandhi, after all, is in bondage to his poverty. He is troubled in conscience at having to contradict his principles by using motor cars, telegraphs, steamships, and mill owners to support his enterprises. The mill owners, on the other hand, are bound by their mills, and the necessity of living on a certain economic level, because the moment they are deprived of the things that money can procure, they are in misery. You are free if you can take poverty, if it comes, and use its limitations as ladders to climb the steeps of God; and you are free if you can take plenty, if it comes, and use it in the purposes of the kingdom of God.

Once while waiting for a train in India, I asked an Indian gentleman if he were going on the train that was due shortly. He replied that he was not, for there were only third-class carriages on it. I told him that I was going on it. "Oh, yes," he replied, "you can go on it, for you are a religious man. If you go first class, it doesn't exalt you, and if you go third class, it doesn't degrade you. You are lifted above these distinctions, but I have to keep them up!" If I had given way to my impulse, I should have danced on the platform! First class doesn't exalt, third class doesn't degrade; pleasure doesn't turn our heads, nor pain break our hearts; plenty doesn't entangle our spirits and poverty, doesn't break them, for we see in them all, an opportunity to use them for the central purposes of our life, which are deeper than any of these things. Poverty and plenty are our life events; the kingdom of God is our life.

Third, the fear of old age. *It is a serious thing to see our physical frame begin to wither and decay.* We may stave it off by subterfuges that science offers in the way of face-lifting and beauty paraphernalia. But it is a losing battle, and in the end, we know that we shall be defeated. This is serious, serious if our life is bound up with our appearances. But suppose it is not? Then, we can look on approaching age with a smile, or, better still, with positive joy. Each period of life offers an opportunity to make a contribution impossible at any other period. In youth, we offered our ardency to God and to man; in approaching age, we shall offer our poise, our experience, our sympathy, qualities which it was impossible to offer at any other age. To grow old, not only gracefully, but gratefully, is the Christian's privilege. For the Christian is not to bear old age, but to use it. Is there anything more utterly beautiful than a face, now grown old, but chiseled into tenderness and sympathy and experience? In forgetting about one's appearance and entering on something deeper, appearances come back, for there is nothing more beautiful in heaven or in earth, than a face that bears the marks of love and purity. "Oh, you with heaven in your face, give me a penny," cried a beggar as he saw the saintly missionary William Pennefather go past.

> *"You are free if you can take poverty, if it comes, and use its limitations as ladders to climb the steeps of God; and you are free if you can take plenty, if it comes, and use it in the purposes of the kingdom of God."*

When I first went to India, it was not easy to get acclimatized, so I came down with fever several times. It was almost worth having fever to have the privilege of the visits of an aged Indian saint called "Caroline Mama." Her face was always suffused with a radiance, and when she arose from her knees after praying by my bedside, she would invariably lean over and leave a kiss upon my fevered brow. As she made her way out of the room, I felt that I had entertained an angel, not unawares, but knowingly. Now, had she been young, she would have timidly inquired at the veranda how I was and would have gone away, but old age has the privilege of going into inner sanctuaries and leaving its kiss where it is most needed. Yes, old age has the privilege of walking into the sanctuaries of the souls of other people, that youth knows nothing about. Old age has its freedoms as well as youth. So, whenever I look into the mirror, and see my hair getting gray, I never feel anything but joy. I shall love it when it is white! For each year of life has been finer than the last, and why should it not be till the end, the end, which is but a fresh beginning?

Among the five hundred gods in one of the temples at Peking, is Marco Polo. The Chinese deified their first visitor from the West. But they made him different from all the others. The Chinese who had been deified, sat in calm poise as though the centuries were looking through their eyes. But Marco was standing, the only one of the five hundred standing, his whole attitude eager, his eyes fierce and glaring, and his face drawn. That was how the poised East looked upon the possessive West. I think I admire more, the generosity of the Chinese in giving Marco a place among the gods, than I do the deification of this restlessness. We of the West, have deified it for so long, and have hoped for so much from it, and have found so little from it, that we do not find ourselves bending the knees before the altar of restlessness as once we did. Another figure of that pantheon interested me more than did Marco Polo, and it left a better taste in my mouth. It was the figure of a man who had been so fine in life, that when he came to old age, his face cracked in the middle, from the forehead down, and he was in the act of pulling off this wrinkled mask, which had behind it the face of youth. He was really young through his goodness, so the outer mask was being stripped away to show his essential self. I loved this old, young man, and saluted him in my heart, for he represented what I felt that the Christian should be, a person who is by the inner renewal of his/her spirit, growing perpetually young.

A very gracious Indian lady was entertaining some foreign visitors in that graceful and beautiful way, so characteristic of the Indian woman. One of the visitors was so impressed with her poise, her dignity, and sweetness that she said in leaving, "You are so beautiful." The Indian lady replied, very quietly, "Why shouldn't I be? I'm seventy-two years of age." She had caught the secret!

Fourth, the fear of death. The chief sufferings of life come from death. We fear death both for ourselves and for those whom we love. We know in a way that it will come to us all, but when it does come, it comes as a surprise and leaves us stunned. I say, "leaves us stunned," but that isn't quite true, for some have learned the secret we have been talking about in this book and it leaves them singing. Almost all the early Christians had caught this note of victory over death. I have just come from the Catacombs of Rome, where two hundred thousand of the early Christians were buried, many of them martyrs. There are many inscriptions on the walls, written by these early Christians, but as far as I can remember there is not a lamentation among them. There is nothing there of the later paganism that filled our graveyards with lamentations about separations and absences. Those Christians believed that Christ had conquered everything, including death, so that there is a solemn joy running through the whole thing. The tone of the inscriptions reminds me of the inscription which the Lees of Calcutta put on the monument set up in

> *"The Christian should be, a person who is by the inner renewal of his/her spirit, growing perpetually young."*

memory of their six children, who were all buried in a landslide one dreadful night on the slopes of the Himalayas at Darjeeling, "Thanks be unto God, which giveth us the victory through our Lord Jesus Christ."

To the Lees and to the early Christians, it was the resurrection of Jesus that gave the whole thing meaning.

The gospel raises the questions that perplex and tear the heart of man in the only way they could be adequately raised, namely, within life itself. Others raised them as philosophies; Jesus raised them as facts. As his twisted body hung on the cross it seemed to turn into a vast question mark against the sky line, and as from his lips comes the cry, "My God, why?" it seems that all the anguish and pain of the ages is gathered up in that bitter cry. There is not a single problem that perplexes and wrings our hearts that is not gathered up in that anguished question. How far can hate go? Why does the universe tolerate injustice? Why are the good seemingly deserted in their hour of anguish? Will the universe back good men? These and many other questions are voiced in that tragic prayer.

What is the answer? The answer must be given in the very place where the questions are raised, namely, in life itself. If the question is raised in connection with matter, the answer, to be an adequate one, must be given in connection with matter. The question was a fact; the answer must be a fact. God did answer, and answer adequately and in the very place where the questions were raised. The cross raises the questions and the resurrection answers them. It answers the fact of injustice and pain with a bigger fact in the victory! It would not have been a complete answer if Jesus had been raised only spiritually, for the questions were raised as physical and spiritual facts, and only a victory that was a victory in both of these realms would suffice. Jesus' resurrection was a victory, a complete and decisive victory, in both of these realms and did, therefore, suffice. God's last word is not the cross, but the resurrection. But that last word is not a spoken word, but a living word, a fact, the most stupendous fact in human history. We know now how things are coming out. God shall speak the last word in human affairs, and that last word will be "Victory." Jesus let life speak its cruelest word, so that the gentlest and purest Heart that ever beat was stilled in death, and then he quietly rose from the dead, came forth from the tomb with the most tremendous words ever uttered upon his lips: "I am the resurrection and the life." It is this that gives the whole thing significance, for it sets the sorrows of life to music and makes the ultimate note to be joy.

God's last word is not the cross, but the resurrection. But that last word is not a spoken word, but a living word, a fact, the most stupendous fact in human history.

Don't tell me that Osiris and other pagan gods had their resurrections, and that the whole thing is taken from the analogy of the coming of the spring from the dead winter. Suppose these stories were current about the resurrections of pagan deities, does that cut the roots of the resurrection of Jesus? No; his roots go too deep to be cut, for they ramify within the very structure of our moral and spiritual universe. Which of the pagan deities backed his resurrection by a life that had sounded the clearest, the deepest, and the most harmonious moral and spiritual notes of the universe? Which of them backed up his victory over death by his victory over life? To believe in a pagan deity rising above death we must see him rising in sinless grandeur above life. Jesus alone backs his victory over death by his victory over life.

"I can actually use the words of myself which Jesus used, 'I and my Father are one,'" said Colonel Olcott, one of the founders of Theosophy, to Carlyle. "Yes," came back the crushing rejoinder, "but Jesus got the world to believe him." Jesus got the world to believe in his resurrection because they saw something more than his resurrection. They saw "the resurrection and the life," and those two, strike exactly the same notes and melt into harmony.

The miracle of Jesus' moral personality, as he rises in sinless grandeur above both saint and sinner, is the central miracle. All the lesser miracles become credible in the light of that central miracle.

When the chief priests and the Pharisees came to Pilate after the death of Jesus, they said, "Sir, we remember that that deceiver said, while he was yet alive, after three days I will rise again. Command therefore that the sepulcher be made sure until the third day, lest haply his disciples come and steal him away, and say unto the people, He is risen from the dead: and the last error will be worse than the first." "The last error," to them the whole of Jesus' life and teaching was an error, he erred or did not fit into their system. Because he did not conform to their pettiness, from their standpoint, it was all an error. But from Jesus' standpoint, their whole spirit and outlook was an error. The ages have been with him! From the standpoint that whatever departs from an established order or system is an error, then the resurrection is an error. Dead men don't rise! The fundamental mistake lies, however, in the assumption that the last and only word lies with the natural order. But did God exhaust his possibilities when he made the natural order? The ease with which things are done in the natural order makes us feel that there are untold possibilities yet unexhausted in God. "This last error" is a departure from the natural order, but it is a departure upward. It is not a recession, a throw-back, but a throw-upward, an evolution hastened. All better acting is an "error" to ordinary standards, but it is an error upward. The resurrection is an error, but it is an error from one standard, namely, the finality of the natural order, to a fitting into the true standard, namely, that of a free and untrammeled God. In that sense it is not error but higher truth. Call it "miracle" if you will. I do not object; for there are at least four great stark miracles or departures in the history of the natural order:

(1) The creation of the spirit of man, here was a departure so amazing that it cannot be called anything less than miracle.

(2) The virgin birth of Jesus-a new beginning on a higher level in humanity.

(3) The resurrection of Jesus, the victory over all lesser life, including death.

(4) The regeneration of an individual man, the bringing up of man into a higher state of being, conforming him to the image of this Higher Man, or, to be accurate, this Higher-than-Man.

These are four stark miracles that usher in new beginnings, beginnings upward. Every single one of them is worthy of the Divine and is what we would expect if there is a good and redemptive God in the universe. If Jesus did not rise from the dead, he ought to have done so! The whole thing would come out wrong if he did not!

For, mind you, the greatest miracle of all is not any of these four: the greatest miracle is just Jesus. The miracle of his moral personality, as he rises in sinless grandeur above both saint and sinner, is the central miracle. All the lesser miracles become credible in the light of that central miracle.

The account says that "Mary Magdalene was there, and the other Mary, sitting over against the sepulcher," saint and sinner sit looking to see what will happen to that sepulcher. If it remains sealed, and there is no victory over death, then humanity sits looking at it, but knows that its hopes are sealed with Him. The crucial hour of human history has come, will goodness and love and life be snuffed out by the forces of evil and hate and death? The answer is, "No! The Lord is risen!" And the ages answer, "He is risen indeed!"

A church-school superintendent and his wife had just lost their child, an only child, and the next Sunday was Easter Sunday. The superintendent went through his duties as usual, but not as usual, for there was a note of triumph and victory about it all. As the pupils walked home that day one boy said very suddenly to his mother,

"They really believe it, don't they?"
"Believe what?" asked the mother.
"Why, the resurrection, and all that."
"Of course; we all believe it."
"Yes," said the boy, very thoughtfully,
"but not that way; they really believe it."

The little fellow saw that the superintendent and his wife were taking hold of the tragedy of death and were transforming it into a triumph of life.

So, when death threatens us and ours, we can say, like the bird that sits upon the twig when the storm threatens to shake it from its branch, "Shake me off; I still have wings." Nothing now can ultimately make us afraid, for we have victory over the ultimate enemy, death. The pain of the bursting of the petals says that the flowers are coming, and the pains of death tell us that the life within us is blooming forth into immortality.

There will be many who will miss in this volume the note of comfort which a loving God gives to his children. I have purposely left it out until this last moment. For if, in dealing with sorrow, the note of comfort is struck as the predominating note, it has a tendency to weaken the fiber of our spiritual natures. God is looked on as the huge Wiper of Eyes. He thus becomes more grandmotherly than good. And we, his hurt children, look on religion more as a comfort-giving power than a character-making power. In that case we miss both the comfort and the character. For there is no real comfort that does not come as a byproduct of spiritual victory within. Nor can character come from spiritual coddling.

There is no real comfort that does not come as a byproduct of spiritual victory within. Nor can character come from spiritual coddling.

"Comfort" comes from two words, *con* "with," and *fortis* "strength," and literally means, "strengthened by being with." Comfort, then, in the New Testament sense, means strength by the companionship of a God who suffers with us. This is a virile comfort. It has iron in it. And that iron is a tonic.

But there is an exquisite sense of comfort from the fact of the presence of a Father who knows and understands and shares all.

I saw a worm, painfully and slow,
But driven by an inward goad,
Assay to cross a dusty road,
Where roaring motors rush and go.
He was destined to be crushed;
His painful end would be the dust.
And how he fared
No one cared.

Am I a worm amid the dust?
Of seeming endless, countless years?
And am I destined to be crushed
Beneath the roll of whirling spheres?
And am I striving for a goal
That I shall never see?
Yearning e'er to be the soul
That I shall never be?
And how I fare
Does no one care?

Something tells me 'tis not so.
Within my heart there is a glow
That makes me smile at fears
Of rolling crashing spheres.
This inner glow is joyous love,
Not for an absent God above;
For here within my heart

Of my very life a part,
My Heavenly Father dwells.
This wondrous fact is what impels
To purer, higher living;
And day by day is giving
The assurance I am not dust,
Nor need I fear I shall be crushed.
And this I know, I shall arrive,
For this dust 'mid which I strive
Once stained the Galilean's feet.
And though brute force crushed him complete,
Till in the dust his bleeding form
Lay like a common, broken worm,
Yet from this very dust did he arise;
And was exalted to the highest skies.
I follow him-possess his life.
Naught do I fear, then, in the strife.
The worlds of matter and evil mind
Strive to break me, my soul to grind-
Let them do their worst or best,
Twill not disturb this inner rest.
I care not what these worlds contrive
For this I know I shall arrive
My Father cares.

Our pilgrimage into the study of the meaning of suffering is over. I trust that we have shown that the gospel of Jesus fulfills, and more than fulfills, the demand of a thoughtful man, when he said that religion "must be able to show that goodness is victorious vitality, and that badness is defeated vitality, that sin is denial, and virtue the fulfillment of the promise inherent in the purposes of man." We have endeavored to show that the same sorrows come upon all, including the Christian, but while they break the spirit of some, they make the spirit of those who have learned his secret. Raphael and the veriest dauber use the same pigments and colors, but one transforms them into a mess and the other into a message. All this pain seems to be necessary if character is the end, for a bird cannot fly except in a resisting medium, and we cannot rise except we rise upon something defeated. We would therefore teach our souls what one father said he would teach his daughter: "And inasmuch as none of us can escape pain, I will teach her that Christian wisdom which elevates us above all suffering and gives a beauty to even grief itself." I trust that we have also got hold of the fact that all this grief and sorrow is not useless:

We have endeavored to show that the same sorrows come upon all, including the Christian, but while they break the spirit of some, they make the spirit of those who have learned his secret.

"That not a worm is cloven in vain;
That not a moth with vain desire
Is shriveled in a fruitless fire,
Or but subserves another's gain."

We have seen that God too, is very deeply involved in all of this, and that his pain subserves our gain. When we see him toiling up a steeper Calvary than ours with the cross upon his back, we know that that cross is intimately and inseparably connected with our redemption.

I trust that we have also learned that God cannot use one unless he knows the wisdom and sympathy won out of pain:

Ah! Must-Designer Infinite!
Ah, Must thou char the wood ere thou canst limn With It?[1]

Yes, it seems as though he must; and when we are being charred in the fires of suffering, we must know that the Infinite Designer is getting us ready to be the instrument of his purpose.

It was said of Jesus that "He took bread, and when he had blessed, he broke it, and gave" it, "took," "blessed," "broke," "gave." That is the order; and if the "breaking" comes before the "giving," we must not wince when we are being broken, for he sees men's needs, and wants to multiply us by the breaking to feed them.

But there is to be no mere passive resignation —-we are to reach out with joy and take hold of whatever comes to turn it for a testimony. The Christian, then, is to be the most incorrigibly happy man on earth, for he has joy "in spite of." His happiness is not dependent on happenings, it is often in spite of happenings. Billy Bray was one of God's troubadours, and he named one of his feet "Glory" and the other "Hallelujah," so that when he walked one of them said "Glory" and the other "Hallelujah." It was a sure instinct for him to

1 Francis Thompson, *The Hound of Heaven,* (1893). Limn is a verb that means to represent or portray. It is most often used to describe the art of drawing or painting a portrait. *Must you burn the wood before you can paint on it?*

name his feet and not the roads, for some of the roads might lead to gardens and some might lead into gloom, but with him the feet still sounded their message, no matter what the road.

Thank God, this way works! It faces all the facts, dodges nothing, uses everything, and shows itself as victorious vitality. A woman went to many shrines in India to find deliverance from the tempests of her spirit. At one of these shrines, a thousand miles from her home, she met a Christian woman who told her of the way through Christ. It seemed incredible, and the woman said so, "You don't know me. Everyone is afraid of my fury. I have laid a curse upon my family in a fit of anger. How can that curse be lifted, and this tempest within me stilled? No, it won't work."

> *We are to reach out with joy and take hold of whatever comes to turn it for a testimony. The Christian, then, is to be the most incorrigibly happy man on earth, for he has joy "in spite of."*

"Try it," said the woman, persisting, for she herself was a joyous illustration of how it did work. The woman went away shaking her head. But a week later in the same pilgrimage place, she came towering through the crowd, and when she saw the woman, she caught her up in her arms and said in a tumult of words: "It works! It works! I tried it. Someone slapped me in the face today and I didn't even want to slap back. Something within me has changed. It works!"

The women stood face to face, sisters of the Great Secret. As they looked into each other's eyes, they knew that they had touched the very center of life, had Life itself, and nothing hereafter could make them afraid. It works!

The Stoic bears, the Epicurean seeks to enjoy, the Buddhist and the Hindu stand apart, disillusioned, the Muslim submits, but only the Christian exults!

WHEN SORROW COMES

It is easy to offer cheap advice to those in sorrow. This pamphlet[1] is not intended as advice. It is rather sharing with you a philosophy of life which I have used for many years. After trying it out under every conceivable circumstance at home and abroad, I find that it works. I literally don't know what it is to have a blue hour or a discouraged one, I haven't had any for years. Is it because I've had no sorrow? I think that I have had the ordinary run of human pain and frustration. If I have found a way to wear it with a smile, and to use it and make it contribute, I would hasten to say that is it is not my way. I learned it from Another. You too can learn it.

I would point out seven "Don'ts," and then seven constructive suggestions. The seven "Don'ts" are hedges we shall put in along the pathway of sorrow to keep us from wandering into bypaths of futility and frustration. Many get caught in these bypaths with dead ends, and

1 Jones wrote *Christ and Human Suffering* in 1933. In 1944, he was asked to write a pamphlet on this same topic. Here we reproduce it its entirety. E. Stanley Jones, *When Sorrow Comes,* (Nashville, TN: The Upper Room Ministries, 1944).

never get anywhere. They uselessly mull over their frustrations and sorrows. Others walk the path of sorrow, refusing tempting bypaths, and then go on to increased usefulness and power.

1. Don't think your case unique.

It can be matched many times over. Sorrow is bound to hit you in some form or other in a world of this kind. Take death, for example. Suppose there were not death. The world would be overcrowded in a few generations. One generation passes away and makes room for another. Death is then not a unique phenomenon, it happens to everybody sometime. But when it occurs within the circle of our love it comes as a surprise. It should not. It is something we all must meet in the normal course of human living.

Take other kinds of sorrow – loss of health, business failure, unhappy home life, the lack of a home, or a life without a partner. These may come from our inhumanity toward each other and partly from the fact that we are living in an imperfect world. We are "the unfinished masters of an unfinished world." With unfinished people in an unfinished world we are bound to have troubles and sorrows. They are bound to come. The question is not their coming, the question is what they do to us when they come. They can make us, or break us. And whether they make us or break us depends upon our inner attitudes.

2. Don't give yourself to self-pity.

The temptation will be to feel sorry for yourself. Don't do that. That will lead straight to introversion, and that will cause the sorrow to fester. If a wound is free from self-pity it will probably heal quickly, but a wound infested with self-pity becomes an infected wound; and an infected wound takes a long time to heal. Keep the virus of self-pity from your wounds. If you allow yourself to pity yourself you will soon be bidding for the pity of others, and if you allow that you'll be in a descending spiral of defeat. A self-pitying self is a pitiable self. Don't allow yourself to slip into that.

3. Don't give yourself to excessive grief.

Many do it, thinking they are thereby showing their love for a departed one. It is a mistake. If the departed loved one could see you, he or she would see how excessive grief causes deterioration of the personality and can ruin your health. To see you deteriorate, would that please the loved one? To see you continuing to love them and loving them so much that it would make them happy to see you radiant and victorious—that would be to show real love.

> *A self-pitying self is a pitiable self. Don't allow yourself to slip into that.*

4. Don't retail your sorrows.

It may be well to talk over your troubles with an understanding friend, to get a trouble up and out is often helpful to relieve the pain. But don't syndicate your sorrows. Don't share them with everybody you meet. They will thereby grow. A friend tells of a boyhood friend who had a sore thumb, and whenever he met anyone he would unwind the big bandage and show the sore thumb. That sore thumb filled his horizon and everybody else's. Every time one of thought him, he thought of a sore thumb sticking up. When people think of you they must not think of sorrow they must think of a person mastering that sorrow. Remember the definition of a bore: "A person who talks about his arthritis when you want to talk about yours."

5. Don't resign yourself to sorrow and feel it will continue.

The probabilities are that unless you keep your sorrow artificially alive it will not continue. Time is a great healer. I have tested this out. Something has hurt me. I feel it deeply. I say to myself: "By tomorrow at this time the pain will automatically be less, it may even be gone." It usually is. The further you are removed from a thing, the less it impacts you for weal or woe.

6. Don't fight against a trouble directly.

To fight against it directly will concentrate your attention on it, and it is a law of the mind that whatever gets your attention gets you. Call your attention away from your sorrow by getting into constructive work for others. That will push the sorrow to the edges. The clenched-fist method of dealing with sorrow fails, for it makes you tense; and when you are tense, the healing, peace-giving power of God cannot get through to you. That power can only come to you through relaxed receptivity.

7. Don't complain.

If you do, your mind will look around for reasons to justify that complaint. If it cannot find reasons it will manufacture them and that will exaggerate the woes and the illnesses, and in so doing will increase them. The more you complain about things, the more things you will have to complain about.

I am sorry that I have to start you off with "Don'ts," but they are the dangers signals set up along the road to victory. We turn now to see how we can walk that road. We will work out seven steps to victory.

1. If suffering has come to you, see whether or not you yourself are the cause of it.

You may not be but then again you may be. It may be that the universe is kicking back in suffering and frustrations because of (1) your own transgressions; and (2) your wrong attitudes toward life. If there are transgressions in your life causing physical, mental, or spiritual disruption, surrender them and lay them at the feet of Christ. You may not be able to overcome them, but you can consent and Christ will do the overcoming. You supply the willingness—He supplies the power. The cause of your suffering and frustration may be in your wrong reactions to life. They may not be classified as transgressions, but they do disrupt the peace and rhythm and health of your life. For instance, I know a person who is suffering from asthma. Whenever he gets into a tight place where he cannot deal with the current situation, he has an asthma attack. The attack lets him down gently. It puts a "pillow" under him so he can fall gently, and save his self-respect. The subconscious mind is saying: "If you were only well you could meet this difficulty, but you are not well and therefore you cannot be expected to meet it—see, you have asthma." The man is unconscious of the fact that his fear and retreatism is a wrong reaction to life, and that it lays the foundation for physical disruptions, in this instance asthma.

Go over your life to see whether you are taking attitudes which are themselves causing disruption and suffering. An intelligent, sympathetic friend may be able to help you get pried loose from wrong attitudes.

2. But your difficulties may not come from your own transgressions and wrong reactions – they may come entirely unmerited.

Jesus made it plain that suffering may not be a sign of sin. He said that the people upon whom the Tower of Siloam fell (the accidents of nature), and the people whose blood Pilate mingled with their sacrifices (the wrong actions of man), were not sinners above the rest. He made room for unmerited suffering. Did He leave it there? Oh, no. He said that unmerited suffering need not merely be borne; *it can be used. Determine, then, to make your sorrows make you—and others.* Here is a positive, active way of dealing with sorrow. You neither escape it, nor merely muddle through it—you use it. Professor James says that "this positive, active way of dealing with sorrow gives a new dimension to life." When life is blocked and frustrated by suffering, there is always a way out, for life has a new dimension. What is this new dimension to life?

It is nothing less that the power to take suffering up into the purpose of your life and transmute it into character and achievement. This is no mere philosophy of life. It is the very essence of the Christian faith – its workable way to life. The idea that the Christian faith offers escape from suffering is completely foreign to that faith. It is true that the Christian way makes you live more in accord with the nature of reality, and therefore you are saved from self-inflicted pain and frustration which comes from barking your shins against the system of things. But while the Christian way saves you from the results of the follies of wrong living, it exposes you to other suffering of a different nature. Society demands conformity. If you fall beneath its standards it will punish you. If you rise above its standards it will persecute you. Society demands an average conformity. But the Christian is a departure upward—she is different. Therefore she is hit because of that difference—she is looked on askance. She is often persecuted. That causes suffering.

There is another cause of the Christian's suffering. Her contract with Christ sensitizes her—she begins to care, and to care on an ever-widening scale. She enters into the sufferings of others and literally makes them her own.

Society demands conformity. If you fall beneath its standards it will punish you. If you rise above its standards it will persecute you.

In addition to these two avenues of suffering, the Christian shares with the rest of humanity the ills incident to life in a world of this kind—death of loved ones, loss of health, loss of friendships, disappointments in love, the nonfulfillment of ambitions, the frustrations that come from living in an unfinished world. In an unfinished world we are bound to meet up with things that balk us, and if we let them they will break us. That is the point—"if we let them." Our reactions to these things largely determine the result. Not what happens to you, but what you do with it after it does happen, determines the result.

The same thing happens to two people, one it makes bitter, the other it makes better. Our inner attitude determines the result.

I have just been in a city where the memory of a man lingers like a beautiful aroma, penetrating everything. That man was Dr. James "Lovely" MacGiffert, a blind mathematician. He taught for many years in a technical college, but in teaching he really taught the science of living. Whenever the alumni asked about their Alma Mater, the first person they asked about was their blind friend and teacher. Dr. MacGiffert taught mathematics, but he made men. One of them had given up all desire for an education and was almost illiterate when a grown man. This blind master of life so inspired and awakened him that he himself is now a professor. The word "Lovely" was affectionately added to his name by his friend, for everything to this blind man was "Lovely," He was always using that word, so they added it to his name. Blindness befell him, and the loveliness of his inner spirit made him and his surroundings "Lovely." That is mastery.

A professor gave a tetanus injection to his little son who had run into a barbed wire. Tragically, the son died in his arms. That might have embittered the couple, but instead it brought them to a decision to dedicate their lives to underprivileged children. That dedication was the branch, which, thrown into the bitter waters of Marah, sweetened them. It was the spirit with which this calamity was met that turned it from a calamity into a consecration.

A famous surgeon and his son were operating on a patient when the father slumped down beside the operating table with a heart attack. The son saw at a glance that nothing could be done for his father, so without a moment's interruption took over from his father and carried on the operation to a successful outcome, and then did what he could for the dead. That son was never so great as when amid the interruption of death, he carried on more faithful service to the living. He had not time for useless, fruitless grief. His best service to his felled father was to carry on where his father left off.

A doctor was attending to the birth of a child when news was brought to him that his wife was dying and that he must get to her at once if he were to see her alive. However, he could not leave the critical situation in which he was, and carried on until the child was safely brought into the world, and then returned home to find that his wife had died. But I am quite sure that his wife would have had him do the very thing that he did, and was deeply proud of him for carrying on.

In both these instances the dedication to something outside of themselves made these men carry over across the spasms of grief into usefulness. Here is another illustration. David Livingstone buries his wife in Africa, and then goes out to find a balm for his broken heart in serving the downtrodden of that land. That is mastery.

There is a saying, "When Fate throws a dagger at you, there are two ways to catch it: either by the blade or by the handle." Fate is bound to throw a dagger at you, no one will be spared. Whether we grasp it by the blade and let it cut us to the quick, or whether we grasp it by the handle and make it an instrument of defense depends on the inner spirit. Our reaction determines the result.

When life threw a cross at Jesus, He took hold of that worst thing that could happen to Him and made it into the best thing that could happen to the world. The cross was sin, pure, unadulterated sin and He turned it into the healing of sin. It was hate, and He turned it into a revelation of love. It was life speaking its darkest, cruelest word, and Jesus turned it into God speaking His most redemptive word. Jesus did not bear the cross, Jesus used it! A religion with a cross at its center doesn't offer mere comfort, a drying of tears, it offers a moral and spiritual mastery that turn sorrow into song and a Calvary into an Easter morning.

3. Remember God is doing with His sorrows exactly what He is asking you to do with yours.

Since God is love, the burdens of love must fall on Him. It is the nature of love to insinuate itself into the pains and sorrows and sins of its loved one. Love takes it on itself and makes what falls on the loved one its own. If this be true, then God is suffering in our suffering, is hurt in our hurts, and wounded in our sins.

And what does God do with His sorrows? He uses them. He makes them redemptive. The cross tells us that. I can worship and love and follow the God of the Nail-pierced Hands. For Jesus is not asking me to do something He is not doing. He shows me how to turn the worst into the best, and to make my very calamities serve. If God redeems the world through a cross, then I can make my sorrows redemptive to myself and others.

4. "Take what you have and make something out of it."

That is the summed-up philosophy of the life of Dr. George Washington Carver, a saint and a scientist, who took slavery, poverty, frustration, and made out of them one of the greatest contribution ever given to American life. Don't cry for what you haven't; take what you have and make it into something else. Joseph took a wrong done to him by his brothers and turned it into the feeding of Egypt and the very brothers who had sold him into slavery. He might have eaten out his heart, chewing on his resentments. He turned a wrong into a glorious right. I know a girl who in spite of a facial deformity has turned her life into one of the most beautiful lives I know. She determined to live in spite of! She is one of the finest youth workers in this country.

There is a famous statue in Mexico by Jesus Garcia, entitled "In Spite Of." The sculptor lost his right hand in the midst of the work on the statue. He determined that he would finish it. He learned to carve with his left hand and finished it, and the carving is better, perhaps, than that he would have done with his right hand. For the quality of life had gone into the statue. So they called the statue, "In Spite Of." When you cannot live "on account of," you can always live "in spite of." When the WWII started someone said to me: "How can you ever be happy again? You tried hard to head off this war, and all your efforts have crashed." My reply, "If I cannot be happy 'on account of,' I can always be happy 'in spite of.'" That possibility is always open.

> *When you cannot live "on account of," you can always live "in spite of."*

Take what you have, and make something out of it. If the thing you have is a sorrow, offer it to God and make out of it a song. If it is an irritation, then do what the oyster does when it gets an irritating grain of sand in its shell, it throws a pearl around it. Make your irritations into iridescences.

5. If you are going to do this, then learn to draw on the resources of God, learn how to pray.

Perhaps you are so blinded by sorrow that you cannot go on alone. True, but you are not alone, you and God can work this out together. Go aside and in the quietness let down the barriers, let go of the tensions, let the healing of God go through every fiber of your hurt soul. God invades you, God heals you, God lifts you up and God give you wings. God makes you into a victorious spirit. *Provided* and this is the point, provided you surrender your sorrow, your frustration into His healing hands. Don't hold on to your sorrow. If you hold it, it will fester within you. Let God have it, forever! Now your pain is "a pain which God is allowed to guide." It is a God-guided pain. A God-guided pain in no longer a mere pain, it is a pain like the pain of childbirth, it is bringing forth something beautiful and significant. It is a fruitful pain. Your very pain, then, becomes a paean.

6. But what if God does not answer my prayers?

What if my prayers are of no avail and my loved one is not restored to health? How can I use the pain of an unanswered prayer?

Perhaps you will have to live on a "but if not." You remember the Hebrew young men about to be cast into a fiery furnace said: "The God whom we serve is able to deliver us from the burning furnace and from your power. But if not, know that we will not bow down the golden image." Note the words, "but if not." Our allegiance to God is not based on this or that answer to prayer, it is based on an allegiance and confidence that can stand the shock of unanswered prayer. For the soul knows that if God doesn't answer this prayer, God is doing so in order to answer a larger prayer, according to a larger plan and purpose. You must not base your faith on a particular answer to a particular prayer for a particular thing. Your faith must rest on confidence in the character of God, your heavenly Father as seen in Jesus Christ. God did not save Him from a cross, but through that cross Jesus saved a world. Suppose His confidence in God had depended upon whether God would or would not save Him and take Him down from the cross? How barren that smaller prayer would have been! How beautiful the larger purpose working through that denial has been! The world has been saved through Jesus not being saved.

You pray that your loved one may be saved from this illness, and you trust he or she will be—"but if not"? Then you go straight on, unbroken in faith and confidence. You pray that your son in war may be spared and brought back to you, and it is right to pray that prayer. "But if not?" If he is not spared? Then you will have to go steadily on, unbroken in confidence. You will have to live on "but if not." Your faith rests not upon this, that, or the other happening, but on something unchanging—the character of God. That always remains. Trust "in spite of," when you cannot trust "on account of."

7. Thank God for your sorrow, even though you cannot understand it now.

When Jesus was about to give the cup to His disciples, the account says, "Having thanked God for it He gave it to them." Into that cup had been poured the wine, the wine with a history. The experiences of the summer, the clouds and the sunshine, the pruning and the cultivating had all gone into the making of that wine. That wine was the symbol of His life. Into the cup of His life which Jesus was pressing to their lips had gone the experiences of the past, the silent years at Nazareth, the struggle in the wilderness, the long nights of prayer and now there was going into it the loneliness of Gethsemane and the rejection and torture of the Cross. Jesus thanked God for all of it, the joys and the sorrow, the triumphs and the bloody sweat—all of it went into the enriching of the cup of His life which He was putting to their lips. The thanking God for it turned the whole thing from a tragedy to a triumph. For it meant that Jesus would use it all.

Into the cup of your life is going all the gladness and beauty, all the pain and disappointments, all the Gethsemane hours and the torturing moments of the cross, it is all going into the enriching of the cup of your life, the cup which you will put to the lips of others. Then thank God for that cup. It is richer for suffering, for suffering triumphed over. The thanks turn it all from a cruel hurt to you to a constructive healing of others through your tragedy.

Mrs. Lee, a missionary in India, lost all of her six children on one night during the monsoon rains when the whole hillside in Darjeeling slipped away and buried them all. She stood up one day in a meeting and said, "I thank God for every sorrow that has come to me." And she meant it! For when their family home was broken apart by the death of their children, they set up a larger home, a home in which, for forty years they had over 300 children living with them. That is moral mastery!

Or take a subtler sorrow—the sorry of having to go through life without a life partner. That sorrow is often the deeper because it is not one that can easily be shared. It is often worn alone in the inner secret of the heart. To have a child and then to lose it is a real sorrow, but not to have had a child at all, that sorrow may be deeper. There are women, many of whom the finest characters in our civilization, who go through life with childless arms and ache to hold a child. Motherhood is denied them. That sorrow can turn them into querulous, bitter, unlovely characters. Or the creative maternal instinct can be sublimated, can be turned into creative art, music, and human sympathy. It can turn the person into a creator of monuments, of constructive good will, or new born souls, or new born hopes in dead souls. In that case the maternal instinct become creative on another level. It is not frustrated, but fulfilled. Then the person can be radiant with usefulness intensified. Some of the greatest contributions to humanity have been made by those, who while unmarried, have married themselves to human need. I sincerely salute that army of brave souls who go on with heads and hearts up and make this world a better place to live in though they themselves are denied parenthood. They save others, themselves they cannot save.

And the bravest of those brave souls are those who thank God for the opportunity of not saving themselves that others might be saved.

You, too, can thank God for your sorrow; not perhaps for the sorrow itself, but for what God is going to do to you and through you because of that sorrow. God is going to help you, not merely to bear it, but to use, it.

COMMENTARY

Whenever I think of my childhood and my parents, I think of their intimate association and loyalty to the Mar Thoma Church in India; going to the Maramon Convention in the late nineteen-forties with my father to listen to Dr. E. Stanley Jones, the author of this book, is part of that pleasant recollection. In 1960, I had the good fortune to attend Dr. Jones' seminars at Waltair, in Andhra Pradesh, in a small group of less than fifty people. I was a student at that time of the Andhra University. At Maramon, I heard him at a great distance, but at Waltair I heard him at very close quarters like a professor giving an intimate tutorial, and I vividly remember him saying that when he was seventy years old he asked God confidently for ten more years to do God's mission, and he was grateful for the life and experience that he had in his journey of life with Christ; he was 76 at that time and lived fruitfully for another thirteen years and died in his beloved India in 1973. Then in 2015, I came across a memoir of him by his granddaughter, Dr. Anne Mathews-Younes, and I was able to publish it as a four part series in the Internet Journal, 'Diaspora FOCUS'. Therefore, I was greatly surprised, but very grateful when Dr. Anne Mathews-Younes asked me to write a commentary for the new edition of 'Christ and Human Suffering', which was initially published in 1933, five years before I was born.

I recount the above experiences as a fitting introduction for my admiration for this 'Missionary Extraordinary' who understood India as no other missionary could and contributed much to establishing the 'Christian Ashram Movement', and providing the spiritual strength and guidance during the freedom struggle as a dear friend of Gandhiji and other national leaders. The book was written when the world was just about recovering from the aftermath of the First World War and was plunging itself into a great economic depression; and India was going through the birth-pangs of the freedom struggle, Nazism was beginning to emerge in Germany and Fascism in Italy. Human sufferings and misery of all kind not only at the level of the individual but also at the communal, national and global level were so depressing and no one could see a way out of this mess. This book was an answer to find a way out using Christ as a guide and a way, the way of Christ. Evil and suffering that existed from within the individual and without at the time of writing this book in the 20th century is still with us in different sizes and shapes and hence this book is a useful guide in addressing these issues, in the way of Christ.

However, the author realised that it would be a risky expedition as he wrote in the introduction to the first edition: "But to write on such a subject is to walk on holy ground, hallowed by the tears and blood-stained footsteps of many wearied one. To bungle here would be serious. To raise hopes in a suffering heart that could not be fulfilled would only add pain to pain. I hesitated. But objection after objection seemed to be swept away, and I came to my final condition and took my stand there, refusing to go on unless I could be assured at this point: I cannot write this book as theory. It must be a working way to live." In the final chapter of this book, we read an amazing testimony from a woman who overcame her sufferings and problems by following the way of Christ and shouted: "It works! It works!" Yes, indeed the human experience of sufferings and joy of overcoming suffering by following the way of Christ is so clearly expressed in thirteen chapters of this book, and it works!

As a skilled physician of the soul, the diagnostic expertise of the author is exemplary and the remedy is equally impressive for the conditions that he witnessed in 1933. The problems that we are facing today are equally depressing such as poverty, mass migration, fear of nuclear war, trade wars, religious intolerance, gender bias, racial intolerance, violence of all kinds, suicides and suicide-bombers, global warming and related ecological issues. His prescriptions are still valid for the problems that we are facing in our world today. We are advised to follow St. Paul's advice: "Carry each other's burdens, and in this way you will fulfil the law of Christ"(Gal. 6: 2). Therefore, we should appreciate and remain grateful to the publishers for reprinting this very valuable book.

The book was organised under thirteen chapters, these chapters overlap and intertwine with one other; it has an overall organic unity. The following is to invite you to enjoy a memorable experience. The first chapter explains various confusing religious and secular ideas about suffering and God's presence or absence in protecting people from such sufferings. The idea that calamity would always only strike the wicked and the righteous would always be saved is questioned. The Christian solution to suffering is not based on such a favourable selective and preferential action of God. If that would be the case then such a protected Christian is nothing but a 'cosmic pet', a spoiled child.

The second chapter deals with the question: "Are Christians spared from suffering?" To find a Christian solution to suffering nine areas of trials and tribulations are identified in Luke's Gospel and discussed at length (Lu. 21: 8-19). The author sums it by saying, "Christ being what he is, and the Christian being what he should be, he is bound to know suffering as the result of following that Christ".

Various ideas of dealing with human suffering in various religions such as Buddhism, Hinduism, Judaism, Islam, and other philosophies are dealt in the third chapter.

Jesus' way of meeting suffering is described through the Gospels in the fourth chapter. Jesus accepts the facts of human suffering, but it is not punishment handed out by God. Jesus' method of meeting pain and injustice is to transform them into something on to a higher plane for the glory of God. "Jesus would turn the world's supreme tragedy into world's supreme testimony", as he did at the cross and at the resurrection. Jesus showed us how to shine by self-sacrifice. Many examples from the Gospels are described here to describe how 'life became luminous as it faced its direst tragedy.' "The cross becomes a throne! The end—a new beginning!"

How early Christians dealt with their suffering in the Christian way is described in the fifth chapter. To these early Christians 'opposition became opportunities,' suffering became songs. They drank 'the new wine of the kingdom.' "They did not bear suffering, or try to escape it—they used it." God refused to heal the infirmity of Paul, but Paul was able to testify that God's grace is sufficient for him. "This refusal to heal is in the interest of a higher good, and then we can accept the refusal as being as much the gift of God as healing." This chapter ends with the note: "The Christian is not spared the pain and sorrows and sickness that come upon other people, but he is given an inner set of the spirit by which he rises above the calamities by the very fury of the calamities themselves."

Chapter Six describes how the Christian way is working in various life situations. The author gives vivid examples of how various people turned their problems to opportunities and gave amazing testimonies of people who transformed their 'Calvaries into Easter mornings.' The author concludes this chapter with the statement: "Christianity is the only religion that throws nothing away—including frustration and pain and suffering. . . . Jesus redeems not only human souls but also fragments that remain when life goes to pieces under the blows of suffering and sorrow and frustration."

Chapter Seven shows us how the Christian way leads us to victory over suffering. The faith of Jesus is like the water Lily or Lotus plant that lays hold of the muck and filth of the pond and transforms itself into beautiful flowers. However, some Christian teachings direct us towards heaven for ending suffering. But heaven should be here and now following the will of God. "Prayer should take us out of the dark corners and help us to turn our infirmities into ladders that reach to heaven here and now." The author says, "The Christian has sufficient resources to meet life no matter how hard the game of life is played against him." In this chapter we see the description of a 'New Testament face' which is a face where 'lines have turned to light, where grief has learnt to smile through its tears, and where, in spite of everything, there is a sense of victory.' Jesus' way does three things: It offers victory over sin, victory over self, and victory over suffering.

The eighth chapter is a detailed study of the two periods of Jesus' life when he was deeply tempted to face the sorrow and sin of the world in some other way than the way of the cross. The first period was coloured by the three temptations immediately after his baptism during his fasting and praying for forty days. Then the second occasion arose from a very brief incident of some Greeks asking Philip for his mediation for them to have a meeting with Jesus in his 'mid-career'. The response of Jesus was simply: "Now my heart is troubled and what shall I say? 'Father save me from this hour'? No it was for the very reason that I came to this hour. Father glorify thy name" (Jn. 12:27). This incidence has great importance according to the author, but it is totally down played by the Gospel writers and theologians through the ages. But if Jesus took the way of the Greeks and followed an Athenian way of life, history would have been totally different. "The Greeks were asking him to love his life and save it, and thus save others; they were asking him to bless without bleeding." But Jesus knew that he should obey the will of his Father and take the way of the cross to save the world. It is a great challenge in a man's life when he has the courage to say no to shortcuts and no to all easy ways, to all compromises and temptation, to go to accept the way of the cross. It is about overcoming evil with good and hate by love, by the way of the cross. "There was no other way, for Jerusalem and the hill called Calvary lay between him and the Easter morning victory." This chapter illustrates and gives an amazing theological insight on this 'Greek route', which I have never come across anywhere else and it is worth pondering on this.

The cost that God paid through Christ for the salvation of humanity is explained in the ninth Chapter and a detailed comparison is made here with the Hindu philosophy of the law of 'Karma'. The cross is the reconciling place between Karma and forgiveness. In Christ we see that God is love. Love is the basis of all redemptive action of God. "Love cannot be love and refuse the burdens of love. In a world like this God cannot refuse the cross and remain a God of Love." The law and love come together in the cross. At creation God assumed a responsibility and in Jesus on the cross God acknowledges and discharges that responsibility. The author concludes: "The crown of life is man, the crown of man is Christ, and the crown of Christ is the cross."

The main thesis detailed in Chapter Ten is how sufferings result from wrong moral choices. Suffering comes from within as a result of our own wrong moral choices and from without as a result of interactions with the environment. However, much of our sufferings come from our own wrong moral choices. "When he lays hold of us within, then all things within us work together for good, for everything then is controlled by the Divine Will. Co-ordinated within, we conquer without." St. Paul says, "And we know that in all things God works for the good of those who love him, who have been called according to his purpose" (Rom. 8:28).

Chapter Eleven deals with the attitude and involvement of society to suffering. Suffering arises from the actions of the individual and from the collective action of society. Therefore, tackling the problem of suffering should deal with the individual and the system that operates it. Therefore, transformation should affect both the individual and the society for the kingdom of God to become a reality. The suffering of the individual must be looked on and felt as the failure of the whole society. A Christian must work to remove the causes of suffering without considering its cost.

The cleansing ministry of Jesus for character formation is described in Chapter Twelve. Jesus cleansed their ideas of God; he reoriented the concept of man; he cleansed life; he cleansed religion; he redefined power; he cleansed suffering and taught vicarious suffering is a gift of God. He emphasised that 'suffering in God is not marginal and accidental, but inherent in the very nature of God as love.' The author says, "God never takes a thing from our hands without putting something better in its place," He quotes Clements of Alexandria: "Christ has turned all our sunsets to sunrises."

'The last word' in the final chapter of this book is about the kingdom of God. The task given to us by Jesus is to accept God's kingdom here on the earth, which he created in the very beginning and declared 'very good'. Now Jesus is asking us to replace the whole present world-order with a new world-order founded on love, sharing and brotherhood. This is God's mission, *Missio Dei,* inaugurated by Jesus and entrusted to the Church. The Christian hope emerging from this is that sin, suffering, and death will be banished from the universe with the ultimate triumph of the kingdom of God. The last part of this chapter deals with four things which people fear most: criticism, material insecurity, old age and death.

Suffering is part and parcel of life. Therefore, the book is about living with individual sufferings—innocent, self-inflicted and inflicted by other agencies; it is about dealing with personal suffering and having empathy and compassion in the suffering of others by growing with Jesus Christ in overcoming them. The style of writing is informal and interactive. The reader engages with illustrations of how other believers followed the way of Christ. These amazing illustrations come from the author's life-long work as a missionary in China and India, from theology, psychology, and above all from real experiences with suffering and tribulations, Jones believed in what we read in Johns' Gospel: "I have said you these things, so in me you may have peace. In this world you will have trouble. But take heart! I have overcome the world" (Jn. 16: 33). I have dealt with pain and suffering all of my professional life—yet gained more profound understanding of it from this book. It is a good companion for everyone and particularly for those who are involved in the ministry of healing. Let us leave the last word to the Indian woman who was asked to follow the way of Christ; she followed Christ's way and shouted: "It works! It works! I tried it. Someone slapped me in the face today and I didn't even want to slap back. Something within me has changed, it works!" Yes, indeed this book works!

Dr. Zac Varghese, FRCPath
Emeritus Professor,
Royal Free Campus, UCL,
London, UK

About the Author

A Portrait of E. Stanley Jones by Shivraj Mahendra
(Asbury Theological Seminary, 2017)

E STANLEY JONES (1884-1973) was described by a distinguished Bishop as the "greatest missionary since Saint Paul." This missionary/evangelist spent seventy years traveling throughout the world in the ministry of Jesus Christ. Jones wrote and spoke for the general public and there is little doubt that his words brought hope and refreshment to multitudes all over the world. As a well-known, engaging, and powerful evangelist, Jones delivered tens of thousands of sermons and lectures. He typically traveled fifty weeks a year, often speaking two to six times a day.

Jones worked to revolutionize the whole theory and practice of missions to third world nations by disentangling Christianity from Western political and cultural imperialism. He established hundreds of Christian Ashrams throughout the world, many of which still meet today. E. Stanley Jones was a crusader for Christian unity, a nonstop witness for Christ, and a spokesman for peace, racial brotherhood, and social justice. He foresaw where the great issues would be and spoke to them long before they were recognized… often at great unpopularity and even antagonism and derision to himself. Many consider Jones a prophet and his honors – and he did receive them – were all laid at the feet of Jesus Christ. Jones would readily admit that his quite ordinary life became extraordinary only because he fully surrendered his life to Jesus Christ!

Jones' writing and preaching did not require people to leave their intellect at the door; his presentation of Jesus engaged both the intellect and touched humanity's desire to experience the living Christ in their lives. When Jones wrote or talked about Jesus, it was as if he knew Jesus personally and could reach out and touch him. Jones described himself as an evangelist… the bearer of the Good News of Jesus Christ. The countless illustrations found in his books and sermons speak to a cross section of humanity and demonstrate, in a multitude of ways, the transformative impact of Jesus Christ on human existence. Few readers or listeners could miss identifying with one story or another – virtually all would find stories that touched their lives. All were offered hope that they, too, could experience the transformation available through self-surrender and conversion.

In presenting Jesus as the redeemer of all of life Jones used his wide ranging study of the non-Christian religions, medicine, psychology, philosophy, science, history, and literature to make the case that the touch of Christ is upon all creation — that the totality of life was created by Christ and for Christ. We were all created to live upon Christ's Way. Jesus' Sermon on the Mount lays out both the principles and the Way.

Jones wrote twenty-seven books. More than 3.5 million copies of his books have been sold and they have been translated into 30 languages. All proceeds from his books have gone into Christian projects. He gave all of his money away! Now more than 45 years after his death — his books and sermons (many written in the 1930s and 40s) are not out of date and with few exceptions are entirely relevant to today's world.

ABOUT THE AUTHOR

According to his son in law, United Methodist Bishop James K. Mathews, "the most salient and spiritually significant characteristics of Stanley Jones were the spiritually transparency, clarity and persuasiveness of his personal witness for Christ. For thirty five years I knew him intimately and had occasion to observe him closely for prolonged periods. He rang true! Once when I asked a Hindu how he was, he replied, 'As you see me.' So it was with Brother Stanley, as he was called. He was as you saw him."

Even after a severe stroke at the age of 88 robbed him of his speech, Jones managed to dictate his last book, *The Divine Yes*. He died in India on January 25, 1973.

Jones' monumental accomplishments in life emerged from the quality of his character cultivated through his intimacy with Jesus Christ. As he lived in Christ, he reflected Christ. That experience is to us when we invite Christ to live in us!

About The E. Stanley Jones Foundation

Our Mission

The E. Stanley Jones Foundation (ESJF) exists to reach today's generations with the life-transforming message of Jesus Christ, and to equip effective Christian evangelism by making available to all, the relevant, rich works of Dr. E. Stanley Jones, whose Christ-centered preaching, teaching, and prolific writings continue to enlighten and bless millions of people worldwide.

Partner with Us

E. Stanley Jones addresses cultural, social, and personal issues in our society and lives today and offers Jesus as "The Way" for a meaningful and abundant life. Please partner with us to tell people about a new type of humanity which lives the principles of Jesus and promises hope with a future. There are many ways you can give such as stock, investment income, gifts from your IRA, including mandatory distributions, outright cash and more. Your gift can be designated for general purposes or one of the following opportunities:

- **Adopt a Jones book** to be updated and published
- **Fund production of a book video** for small group study
- **Underwrite the creation of a children's book**
- **Fund a teaching guide** for a Jones book
- **Fund the production of a quality documentary about the life and ministry of E. Stanley Jones**

Email jennifer@estanleyjonesfoundation.com or call 240-328-5115 for more information about these gift ideas.

The E. Stanley Jones Foundation is a nonprofit 501(c)(3) organization. The United States Internal Revenue Service Code permits the amount that US residents donate, which exceeds the fair market value of the goods or material(s) a donor receives from the Foundation, to be tax-deductible.

Two Ways to Give and Partner with Us

Give online at www.estanleyjonesfoundation/donate
or send your gift to:

E. Stanley Jones Foundation
10804 Fox Hunt Lane
Potomac, MD 20854

Our Phone: 240.328.5115

Thank you for helping people discover Christ.
Your generosity is appreciated.

Follow us on social media:

Books by E. Stanley Jones

The following book list is in chronological order according to the date each was written by Jones.

The Christ of the Indian Road
Christ at the Round Table
The Christ of Every Road
The Christ of the Mount
Christ and Human Suffering
Christ's Alternative to Communism
Victorious Living
The Choice Before Us
Along the Indian Road
Is the Kingdom of God Realism?
Abundant Living
How to Pray
The Christ of the American Road
The Way
Mahatma Gandhi
The Way to Power and Poise
How to be a Transformed Person
Growing Spiritually
Mastery
Christian Maturity
Conversion
In Christ
The Word Became Flesh
Victory Through Surrender
A Song of Ascents
The Reconstruction of the Church
The Unshakable Kingdom and the Unchanging Person
The Divine Yes

BOOKS BY E. STANLEY JONES

All publications are available for purchase at:

www.estanleyjonesfoundation.com
www.amazon.com
www.cokesbury.com

Proceeds from the sale of books and materials remain in the E. Stanley Jones Foundation to continue the ministry and fulfill the mission of the Foundation.
Volume pricing for books is available by contacting the E. Stanley Jones Foundation.

Recent Publications by the E. Stanley Jones Foundation

THE 21ST CENTURY EDITION SERIES
VICTORY
THROUGH SURRENDER
E. STANLEY JONES

A LOVE AFFAIR
WITH INDIA
The Story of the Wife And Daughter of
E. Stanley Jones
Preface by Anne Mathews-Younes

LIVING UPON THE WAY
SELECTED SERMONS OF
E. STANLEY JONES
Anne Mathews-Younes

Conversion
E. STANLEY JONES

THE
UNSHAKABLE
KINGDOM
AND THE
UNCHANGING
PERSON
E. STANLEY JONES

A HISTORY OF THE
SAT TAL
CHRISTIAN ASHRAM
Anne Mathews-Younes

IN
OUR
TIME
The Life and Ministry of
E. STANLEY JONES
Robert G. Tuttle, Jr.

CHRIST
AT THE
ROUND TABLE
E. STANLEY JONES

GROWING
SPIRITUALLY
E. STANLEY JONES
Timothy C. Tennent, PhD

TAILWIND
The Robert E. Miller Story
Jennifer Tyler
Nicholas Younes

Christ's Alternative...
E. STANLEY JONES
MARCIA GRAHAM
DR. JOSEPH B. KENNEDY, SR.

THE WAY TO
POWER
and POISE
E. STANLEY JONES
Dr. William O. (Bud) Reeves

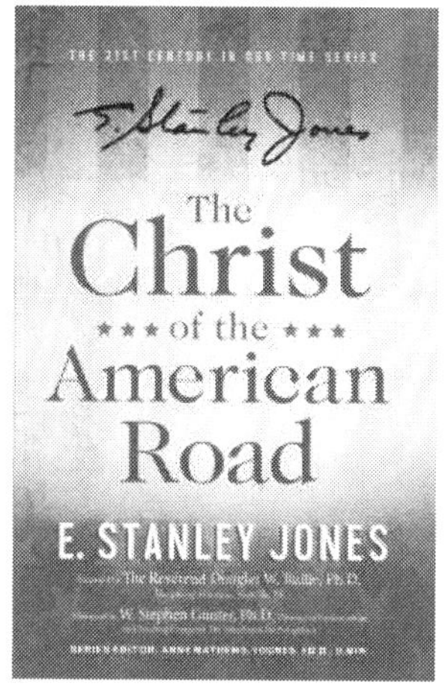

The E. Stanley Jones Quotes Perpetual Calendar

Calendar only available through the E. Stanley Jones Foundation bookstore

The New Testament Poster

Jones and the Artist

Jones traveled globally with this picture for years and often displayed it when he spoke. According to E. Stanley Jones God revealed himself first through his creation, then through the Bible, and finally through the perfect revelation of his son, Jesus. The full message of God can only be conveyed in the Person of Jesus. In Christ, God gave us a Person, not a word. Jones concluded that Christianity was unique for it was God's search for man and God came to us in a Person. Christianity is the divine Word became Flesh—and that makes all the difference in the world.

This picture was created by a Korean artist, (a refugee from North Korea) for Jones. The uniqueness of the picture is that the whole of the New Testament is written from corner to corner beginning with the Gospel of Matthew and ending up with the book of Revelation. It is all written in minute letters by hand in English. There are 185,000 words in the picture—about a thousand words on a line.

The picture took the artist two years to create and the words are so minute that most people cannot read them with the naked eye. Note that the artist hasn't imposed the figureof Jesus on the words, but he has inked the words light or dark to bring out the form and figure of Jesus. So that out of the words arise the Word. In talking about the picture, Jones said, "These words take us beyond the words to the Word—the Word made Flesh. Out of the Gospels arises the Gospel. Jesus was the Gospel. He didn't come to bring the Gospel. He was the Gospel. The Gospel lies in His person. He himself is the Good News. This painting illustrates that the Gospel lies in the Person of Jesus."

There are twenty-seven little figures (angels) around the edges of the picture. The little angels represent the twenty-seven books of the New Testament all looking at Jesus. The whole of the Christian Gospel then is converging in this Person.

A lithograph of this incredible New Testament Poster is available on the E. Stanley Jones Foundation website in the bookstore. www.estanleyjones.com

The year 2025 marks the 100th Anniversary that the Methodist Publishing House has had at least one Jones book in print and circulation.

Made in the USA
Middletown, DE
25 July 2024

57969815R00135